Editors' Preface to Macmillan Studies in Economics

The rapid growth of academic literature in the field of economics has posed serious problems for both students and teachers of the subject. The latter find it difficult to keep pace with more than a few areas of their subject, so that an inevitable trend towards specialism emerges. The student quickly loses perspective as the maze of theories and models grows and the discipline accommodates an increasing amount of quantitative techniques.

'Macmillan Studies in Economics' is a new series which sets out to provide the student with short, reasonably critical surveys of the developments within the various specialist areas of theoretical and applied economics. At the same time, the studies aim to form an integrated series so that, seen as a whole, they supply a balanced overview of the subject of economics. The emphasis in each study is upon recent work, but each topic will generally be placed in a historical context so that the reader may see the logical development of thought through time. Selected bibliographies are provided to guide readers to more extensive works. Each study aims at a brief treatment of the salient problems in order to avoid clouding the issues in detailed argument. Nonetheless, the texts are largely self-contained, and presume only that the student has some knowledge of elementary micro-economics and macro-economics.

Mathematical exposition has been adopted only where necessary. Some recent developments in economics are not readily comprehensible without some mathematics and statistics, and quantitative approaches also serve to shorten what would otherwise be lengthy and involved arguments. Where authors have found it necessary to introduce mathematical techniques, these techniques have been kept to a minimum. The emphasis is upon the economics, and not upon the quantitative methods. Later studies in the series will provide analyses of the links between quantitative methods, in particular econometrics, and economic analysis.

MACMILLAN STUDIES IN ECONOMICS

General Editors: D. C. ROWAN and G. R. FISHER

Executive Editor: D. W. PEARCE

Published

John Burton: WAGE INFLATION
Miles Fleming: MONETARY THEORY
C. J. Hawkins and D. W. Pearce: CAPITAL INVESTMENT APPRAISAL
C. J. Hawkins: THEORY OF THE FIRM
David F. Heathfield: PRODUCTION FUNCTIONS
Dudley Jackson: POVERTY
P. N. Junankar: INVESTMENT: THEORIES AND EVIDENCE
J. E. King: LABOUR ECONOMICS
J. A. Kregel: THE THEORY OF ECONOMIC GROWTH
George McKenzie: THE MONETARY THEORY OF INTERNATIONAL TRADE
S. K. Nath: A PERSPECTIVE OF WELFARE ECONOMICS
Antony Peaker: ECONOMIC GROWTH IN MODERN BRITAIN
D. W. Pearce: COST-BENEFIT ANALYSIS
Maurice Peston: PUBLIC GOODS AND THE PUBLIC SECTOR
Nicholas Rau: TRADE CYCLES – THEORY AND EVIDENCE
David Robertson: INTERNATIONAL TRADE POLICY
Charles K. Rowley: ANTITRUST AND ECONOMIC EFFICIENCY
C. H. Sharp: TRANSPORT ECONOMICS
G. K. Shaw: FISCAL POLICY
R. Shone: THE PURE THEORY OF INTERNATIONAL TRADE
Frank J. B. Stilwell: REGIONAL ECONOMIC POLICY
John Vaizey: THE ECONOMICS OF EDUCATION
Peter A. Victor: ECONOMICS OF POLLUTION
Grahame Walshe: INTERNATIONAL MONETARY REFORM
E. Roy Weintraub: GENERAL EQUILIBRIUM THEORY

Forthcoming

R. W. Anderson: ECONOMICS OF CRIME
G. Denton: ECONOMICS OF INDICATIVE PLANNING
D. Fisher: MONETARY POLICY
J. A. Kregel: THEORY OF CAPITAL
Richard Lecomber: ECONOMIC GROWTH AND ENVIRONMENTAL QUALITY
David J. Mayston: THE IDEA OF SOCIAL CHOICE
Simon Mohun: RADICAL ECONOMICS
B. Morgan: MONETARISM AND KEYNESIANISM
Christopher Nash: PUBLIC *v.* PRIVATE TRANSPORT
F. Pennance: HOUSING ECONOMICS
M. Stabler: AGRICULTURAL ECONOMICS
J. van Doorn: DISEQUILIBRIUM ECONOMICS
E. Roy Weintraub: THE ECONOMICS OF CONFLICT AND CO-OPERATION
J. Wiseman: PRICING PROBLEMS OF THE NATIONALISED INDUSTRIES
A. Ziderman: MANPOWER TRAINING: THEORY AND POLICY

Trade Cycles: Theory and Evidence

NICHOLAS RAU

Lecturer in Political Economy,
University College London

Macmillan

First published 1974 by
THE MACMILLAN PRESS LTD
London and Basingstoke
Associated companies in New York Dublin
Melbourne Johannesburg and Madras

SBN 333 15241 7

Printed in Great Britain by
THE ANCHOR PRESS LTD
Tiptree, Essex

Contents

Preface

The trade cycle has been a central feature of the history of capitalist economies; it is in the context of this experience that most of our knowledge of stabilisation policies has been developed; and the forecasts, made a few years ago, of the obsolescence of the cycle look rather dated in their optimism.

My main reason for writing this book is that much important work has been done in the last fifteen years, particularly on econometric models and on monetary factors in the cycle, which needs to be brought to the attention of a wider audience. But I have also two more general reasons. First, even third-year students in economics seem remarkably ignorant of dynamics; in Chapter 2 of this book I attempt to give an account of some standard macro-dynamic models which is reasonably simple without being grossly fallacious. Second, I hope that some students who regard applied and theoretical macro-economics as two quite distinct and unrelated subjects will be moved by this book to see the error of their ways.

Trade cycle textbooks in the 1950s tended to devote several chapters to national income accounting, consumption functions, and other topics now well treated in dozens of general textbooks on macro-economics. I have perhaps gone to the other extreme in eschewing 'general macro' subjects. The reader should note in particular that Chapter 5 discusses monetarism and its critics only in so far as the controversy is relevant to trade cycles.

The main economic prerequisite for reading this book is a basic grounding in macro-economics at about the level of D. C. Rowan's *Output, Inflation and Growth* (Macmillan, 1968; 2nd edn 1974) – in other words, slightly beyond the usual British first-year university course, but not much. The only mathematical prerequisites are simple algebra, the ability to handle inequalities, and patience. Chapter 2 states without proof, and explains, the relevant results on difference equations. Complex numbers and differential equations are not explicitly used. Some small knowledge of probability and statistics will be helpful for Chapter 4.

Professor G. R. Fisher and Mr D. W. Pearce read the first draft with great care, and I am grateful to them for numerous suggestions. I am indebted to Mrs I. M. Gayus for her very efficient typing of the manuscript. My greatest debt is to my mother, whose assistance with innumerable chores vastly increased my ability to concentrate on writing. This book is dedicated to her with love and gratitude.

1 The Nature of Trade Cycles

Let us begin on a note of confusion. British economists speak of 'trade cycles', rarely of 'business cycles'; American economists write about 'business cycles', seldom about 'trade cycles'; indeed, Americans tend to use 'trade' as shorthand for 'international trade', not for 'economic activity'. Today the British economist writing about a 'trade cycle' means essentially the same thing as his American counterpart would mean by a 'business cycle', although this was not strictly true in the past. In this book, the terms are used synonymously.

The term 'trade cycle' is intended to describe a class of historical events. It is not a well-defined relationship between economic variables, such as a demand curve. Thus, no definition of a trade cycle is going to be both helpful and precise. Here are two, taken from leading American authorities:

> A cycle consists of expansions occurring at about the same time in many economic activities, followed by similarly general recessions, contractions and revivals which merge in the expansion phase of the next cycle: this sequence of changes is recurrent but not periodic...
>
> (W. C. Mitchell [38] p. 468)

and

> cycles are...recurring alternations of expansion and contraction in aggregate economic activity, the alternating movements in each direction being self-reinforcing and pervading widely all parts of the economy.
>
> (R. A. Gordon [19] p. 249)

Now consider the irreverent question: do these quotations say anything more than 'sometimes national income goes up and sometimes it goes down'? I think they do, for two reasons.

11

First, both definitions emphasise the widely diffused character of expansions and contractions, with the major sectors of an economy moving up and down more or less together. There is clearly no *arithmetical* reason why a 5 per cent expansion of industrial production should not be generally associated with a 15 per cent increase in the production of one half of industry, together with a 5 per cent *decline* in the production of the other half. Indeed, the long-term process of innovation and economic growth has been accompanied throughout the last two centuries by substantial declines of large industries. The fact that this is *not* the typical pattern in the shorter-term fluctuations with which this book is concerned, is clearly something which the economist needs to explain. The post-Keynesian economist will naturally regard the multiplier as having a large part to play in the explanation.

Second, the former quotation mentions 'phases', the latter the 'self-reinforcing character' of expansion and contraction. This suggests that cycles have a certain shape to them which, though not repeated exactly through time, makes a graph of national income or industrial production against time look very different from a merely haphazard mess of fluctuations.

To put this point more technically, there is a lot of difference between a random process and a random walk. A random process is any sequence of events in which pure chance, as well as mechanical or deterministic factors, plays a role. A random walk is the very special case of a random process displayed, for example, by the drunkard who may at any moment move one step forward (with probability, say, 0·5), stay still with a probability of 0·3, or take a step backwards (probability 0·2); he will (almost) certainly get home to his wife eventually, but his behaviour at any one time depends *purely* on chance and not at all on where his position happens to be on the road from the pub to his home. The point of this analogy is that, in reality, *all* economic phenomena are random *processes*, even though they may not be treated as such in economic theory. Indeed the importance of random shocks in the generation of cycles will be heavily emphasised in Chapter 4. On the other hand, there is no evidence that either G.N.P., or G.N.P. *per capita*, or G.N.P. adjusted for trend, or the rate of growth of G.N.P., has

12

moved in a mere random *walk* through time in any advanced capitalist country. On the contrary, the evidence suggests that these variables have been in part systematically determined and in part determined by chance.

We now introduce some common terms of trade-cycle analysis with the aid of Fig. 1, which shows some measure of income (G.N.P., industrial production) plotted against time. The figure describes two successive cycles. The first (depicted

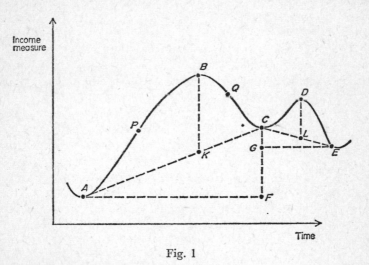

Fig. 1

by *ABC*) starts at the *trough A*, has *expansion* phase *AB*, has the *peak* at *B*, its *contraction* phase *BC* and ends at the trough *C*, which is also the start of the next cycle (*CDE*). The *trough-to-trough length* of the cycle *ABC* (measured in units of time) is the time interval from the occurrence of *A* to that of *C*, and is therefore measured by the *horizontal* distance *AF*. Similarly, the trough-to-trough length of the second cycle is the length of the horizontal line *GE*: thus the first cycle is longer than the second. Also, note that the amount by which income changes in the course of cycle *ABC* is, by any yardstick, more than for the second cycle; in technical language, the *amplitude* of *ABC* exceeds the amplitude of *CDE*. There are various ways of measuring amplitude, not all of which give the same ranking

13

for different cycles; one way is to draw a line between the two troughs and let the amplitude be the vertical (*not* perpendicular) distance between the peak and that line. According to this definition of amplitude, the amplitudes of the cycles in Fig. 1 are the distances *BK* and *DL*.

Much other terminology is used to describe the phases of a cycle. Peaks and troughs are sometimes called 'upper and lower turning points'. Another term for an expansion is the *upswing*, and for a contraction, the *downswing*. The words 'boom',

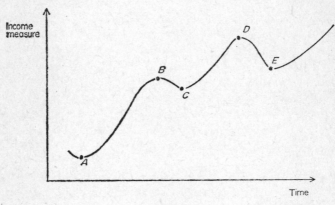

Fig. 2

'slump' and even (probably) 'recession' are perhaps best avoided in scientific discourse, mainly because the logical confusion between 'high' and 'rising' has meant that these terms have ceased to mean very much. Is a 'boom' the same thing as an expansion (*AB*), the latter stages of an expansion (*PB*) or a period of high income *both before and after* a peak (*PQ*)? My guess is that one could find proponents of all three interpretations.

Figure 1 is in one respect misleading. This is because cyclical behaviour in economic activity has generally taken place in the context of a growing economy. Cycles, in the United States and western Europe, have been *fluctuations about a rising trend*. This means that a snapshot of two cycles in a real economy is likely to look more like Fig. 2 than Fig. 1. Fig. 2, being a picture

14

of two cycles in a growing economy, displays one of the important features of historical cycles: that contractions tend to last for a shorter time than expansions. To these and other facts we now turn.

For over fifty years the National Bureau of Economic Research in New York has been analysing cyclical behaviour in the United States and European economies. A major part of its effort has been to build up a detailed chronology of the different phases of expansion and contraction, using a vast mass of carefully collected statistical material on economic time series, in the form of indices and indicators. While the National Bureau's placing of turning points for particular cycles is sometimes disputed, its volumes are regarded by most economists almost as an embodiment of what is known about cycles.

According to the National Bureau, the United States economy underwent 25 business cycles between 1857 and 1960. Their length (trough to trough) varied from 28 to 99 months, with an average of 49 months; the average length of expansions was 30 months, of contractions 19 months. In Britain, cycles tended to be longer at least before the Second World War: in the period from the mid-nineteenth century to 1939 the average length of British trade cycles, again according to the National Bureau classification, was 64 months. Again, the variability of the cycle length was considerable, the interval from one trough to the next ranging from 28 to 102 months. Other European countries seem to have shared with Britain the feature of longer cycles than the United States: in the period 1879–1932 there were 15 cycles in the United States, 11 each in Britain and France and only 10 in Germany. Since the Second World War, European cycles seem to have become shorter; this is particularly noticeable in Britain, where the American four-year pattern has, since 1950, become more marked. This may be due to political factors, and will be remarked on further in Chapter 6.

Just as the length of cycles in any one country varied considerably over time, so has amplitude. Burns [9] illustrated this by considering the 10 cycles in the United States economy between 1919 and 1960. The percentage increase of industrial production during expansions varied from 18 per cent to 93 per

15

cent, the percentage decline during contractions from 7 per cent to a staggering 66 per cent during the terrible years from 1929 to 1933.

The evidence on the timing of cycles produced by the National Bureau is by no means confined to broad aggregates such as income and employment: herein lies much of its importance. Also, there seem to be quite clear patterns by which certain parts of the economy show evidence of an increase in activity before such an increase becomes general and otherwise which are slow, so to speak, to jump on to the expansionary bandwagon after it has started to move, and slow to jump off it after others have done so. Evidence for the United States economy suggests, for instance, that orders for machinery and investment in inventories of raw materials tend to 'lead' the cycle (for example, to fall before G.N.P. has reached its peak) while plant and equipment investment and *aggregate* stock-building tend to lag behind.

Just as differences in timing between different indices of economic activity tend to be repeated in successive cycles, so do differences in amplitude. Profits and investment are prone to particularly large fluctuations; industrial production fluctuates in a wider range than does *total* output, which in turn fluctuates more than personal income.

Many of these tendencies may seem rather obvious consequences of well-known engineering and institutional facts. The lead–lag structure of different types of industrial production may reflect merely the techniques of production; the differences in amplitude between different measures of 'income' and 'output', the operation of the social security system or the non-cyclical and indeed counter-cyclical behaviour of all public works (and it should be noted that this last phenomenon goes back a long way before Keynes). But it is of course important to know just how reliable the pattern is, both for purposes of prediction (is a recovery under way, or is it a false alarm?) and to see whether departures from the pattern do mark a radical break from the past.

Cycles do not simply repeat themselves. Thus there are counter-examples, within American business-cycle history over the last century and a half, to almost any general proposition one cares to make. For example, we might say that expansions last longer than contractions; this is largely true, but the 1873–9 contraction lasted longer than any expansion before 1960. It is usually true that interest rates rise in expansions; but interest rates declined in 1933–7. And so one can go on.

To complicate matters still further, it should not be thought that trade cycles as chronicled by the National Bureau, or even fluctuations remotely like them, are the sole cyclical movements that observers have been able to detect in the economic activity of industrial nations. The last paragraph implied that cycles would be complicated animals even if all that happened in economic history was a (roughly) four-year cycle superimposed on a steady upward trend. But the true picture is far more that of one cycle imposed on another cycle and so on.

For a start, there are numerous cyclical movements of a purely seasonal variety; the Christmas shopping spree is an example. These are not of great importance for the 'armchair' economist, though they are, of course, relevant to the economic statistician trying to sort out cyclical influences from purely seasonal ones.

Longer than the seasonal effects but still shorter than the National Bureau cycle is the 18–21 month 'sub-cycle', believed by some National Bureau economists to exist in the United States. This is mainly the result of the accumulation and decumulation of inventories (stocks).

As well as very short cycles, there are, it has been claimed, very long ones. Some economists, including Schumpeter [46], have expressed belief in a 55-year 'Kondratieff' cycle whose upswings correspond to major innovations, and whose contractions are long periods of relative stagnation. But there is rather little evidence for the existence of such cycles.

More serious are the so-called 'Kuznets' cycles ('long swings', 'building cycles'), 16–20 years in length, usually associated with changes in construction activity. These were certainly a reality in the nineteenth-century United States, and something of the kind also went on in Europe, although it is interesting to note that the European cycle is out of phase with the United States cycle. The cycles would appear to have been strongly related to migration (which would account for the lack of

17

phase). For this reason, and because of the increasing diversification of United States domestic investment, they are, according to Abramovitz [3], extinct in the United States. There certainly seems to be little sign of them in recent statistics, whether for these or for other reasons. Whether western European economies are still strongly affected by a Kuznets cycle is something that would bear investigation.

The concept of 'major cycles', roughly twice the length of the average National Bureau cycle and co-existing therewith, has long appealed to many economists and economic historians. According to this classification, the two cycles of Fig. 2 would be regarded as *one* 'major cycle', with troughs at A and E and a peak at D. Proponents of this idea were Schumpeter (with his 'Juglar' cycle of 8–10 years in length) and Alvin Hansen, whose reading of United States data revealed to him 17 cycles between 1795 and 1937 with average length (peak to peak, this time) of 8·5 years. Perhaps the clearest exponent of the major cycle idea is W. W. Rostow, who in his work on nineteenth-century British trade cycles ([42] chapter 2) first found, by the National Bureau method, 24 cycles between 1790 and 1914 with an average length of 5·25 years. But a reorganisation of his evidence into major cycles, distinguished by nearly full employment at the peak and massive investment in the latter stages of expansion, gave a very steady pattern of major cycles with a consistent duration of about nine years. Rostow in fact goes further than this and distinguishes major and minor cycles by their motive forces, which he believes to have been long-term industrial investment for the former, export fluctuations for the latter.

The 8–10 year cycle, then, may be regarded as *the* classical English trade cycle of the nineteenth century; and Matthews [35] found that United Kingdom data also revealed two such cycles (peak to peak) for the years 1920–37. But in the same work, and using the same methods, Matthews indicated that a much shorter cycle length was apparent from the post-war data.

For the rest of this book, 'the cycle' will mean something like the National Bureau cycle. In the last chapter we shall raise the issue of whether even this exists any more, or whether enlightened stabilisation policies have suppressed it in the post-war era.

But to organise one's thoughts about the dynamics of an economy in aggregate, one needs a dynamic macro-economic theory. The next item on the agenda is to discuss this.

Guide to further reading
A good general description of trade cycles is given in A. F. Burns' survey [9]. Details of the National Bureau's method of measurement are spelt out in the massive classic by Burns and Mitchell [10]. Koopmans' brilliant review article [30] on Burns and Mitchell gives a short but helpful description of their methods and a severe critique of their 'unbendingly empiricist' approach. (To appreciate the prophetic character of Koopmans' 1947 article, read it after Chapter 4 of this book.)

For a brief, readable discussion of British cycles in the nineteenth century read Habakkuk [21]; for more recent British experience see Matthews ([36], Chapter 12; and [35]).

Kuznets cycles are a fascinating topic; good articles are by Abramovitz ([2], [3]), O'Leary and Lewis [40], and in a more sceptical vein by Adelman [4] and Howrey [27].

2 Dynamic Income–Expenditure Models

In this chapter we introduce some of the theoretical ideas, tools and techniques which are repeatedly applied in modern work on stabilisation policy and the econometric analysis of trade cycles. We shall discuss dynamic models of income determination, stocks and stock-adjustment, some mathematics of difference equations and the fundamental properties of multiplier–accelerator interaction.

The purpose of this is to acquaint the reader with the language and method of the later sections of this book, and of the research literature, rather than to present a complete theory of the trade cycle. Indeed, of our three illustrative models, the first is incapable of giving rise to cycles, and the other two are 'cyclical' only in a rather unsatisfactory sense.

Each of the three models considered is a truly dynamic extension of the income–expenditure model of the elementary textbooks; in each model the aim is to investigate the behaviour of aggregate income over time, under specified assumptions. Before the models themselves are introduced, the terms 'truly dynamic' and 'income–expenditure model' must be explained.

A dynamic model is a set of equations purporting to describe the behaviour of some system through time, and which involves time explicitly. Time can be treated in either of two ways: by splitting it up into discrete periods, or by treating it as a continuous variable. This book uses only the 'discrete-time' approach; the 'unit period' in the stylised models of this chapter and the next may be thought of as a month or a quarter.

In economics it is convenient to make a distinction between 'truly dynamic' (or 'causal') models and what we call here 'bogus-dynamic' models. A truly dynamic model is distinguished

23

by the property that the value of each variable at time t is determined by the decisions of a particular agent or group of agents identified explicitly within the model, and not determined invisibly 'through the market' by what appears to be instantaneous price or quantity adjustment.

All the income–expenditure models below are truly dynamic. To give an example of 'bogus' dynamics consider one formulation of the familiar 'cobweb' model of Supply (S) and Demand (D) for a commodity (price p). Subscripting variables by the relevant time periods, we have

$$S_t = a + bp_{t-1}$$
$$D_t = c - dp_t$$
$$S_t = D_t$$

This is a dynamic model, since p_t and p_{t-1} both appear explicitly. It is not, however, causal. For consider the market at the beginning of period t. Since supply has been fully determined by price at $t-1$, the short-run supply schedule for period t is vertical. The demand curve is, of course, downward-sloping. The model asks us to believe that price adjusts *within period t* so as to equate supply and demand; how, and how quickly, it does so is not explained. Of course, certain prices do adjust very quickly to clear markets; the object of the discussion is not to criticise the model on grounds of lack of realism or to attack equilibrium economics, but simply to point out that this formulation of the cobweb is bogus-dynamic in respect of the dynamic adjustment process. The virtue of truly dynamic models comes not so much from realism as from clarity; causal models tell a story of the dynamic adjustment path to equilibrium – bogus-dynamic ones do not.

By an 'income–expenditure model' is meant a description of short-run behaviour of the main aggregates in an economy (assumed closed) ignoring (for the moment) both monetary factors and supply constraints. Adjustment is assumed to take place through the responsiveness of aggregate demand to income and changes thereof, and through the responsiveness of output to aggregate demand.

The main aggregates with which we are concerned (all subscripted to period t) are:

24

$C_t \equiv$ consumption demand, $I_t \equiv$ Investment demand
$Z_t =$ aggregate demand $= C_t + I_t$ and $Y_t \equiv$ aggregate income.

Note that, as an accounting identity, $Y_t \equiv$ aggregate output. Y_t and Z_t, on the other hand, are *not* identically equal, for demand can be met by running down stocks, or may simply not be met. Similarly an excess of production over demand will imply *unintended* inventory accumulation, which is not part of I_t.

In what units are C_t, I_t, Z_t, and Y_t measured? Some 'real' income measure is clearly appropriate, but there are two ways of doing this. One is the way conventional in the textbooks, of deflating money income by a price index. The other is the approach of Keynes's *General Theory*, of measuring quantities in wage units, that is by deflating by an index of money wages. For our purposes, either interpretation will do.

Similarly the assumption that monetary factors are to be ignored can be given a dual interpretation. One may be summarised in the phrase 'money doesn't matter'. The other is to say that the only way in which monetary occurrences affect the 'real' economy is through 'the' interest rate, and that we imagine the interest rate is held constant by the monetary authorities. These assumptions are unlikely to be compatible with each other in any economy in which changes in expectations of the inflation rate play a large role, but they will do for the present.

Finally we must recall the assumption that we are ignoring supply constraints, and dealing only with the short run. This means two things: first, bottlenecks and labour shortages are ignored; and second, that *the only relevance of 'I' is as a component of aggregate demand, not as the expansion of the economy's productive potential through capital accumulation.*

Now we can deal with the models themselves.

MODEL A. THE DYNAMIC MULTIPLIER WITH CONSUMPTION LAG

The assumptions of this model are

Consumption function

$$C_t = a + mY_{t-1} \quad \text{where } 0 < m < 1 \qquad \text{(A1)}$$

Investment function

$$I_t = \bar{I} \quad \text{(a positive constant)} \qquad \text{(A2)}$$

Output determination

$$Y_t = Z_t \quad (= C_t + I_t \text{ by definition)} \qquad \text{(A3)}$$

Thus consumption depends on last period's income, with marginal propensity to consume 'm', and investment is constant through time. Notice that (A3) is *not* an accounting identity but states the strong assumption that output responds without lag to aggregate demand. Note that this instantaneous response does not make the model 'bogus'; for what the producers are responding to are consumption and investment decisions made by agents in the previous period.

From (A1), (A2) and the definition of Z_t, we get

$$Z_t = a + \bar{I} + mY_{t-1} \qquad \text{(A4)}$$

Defining
$A = a + I =$ total autonomous expenditure, and eliminating Z_t between (A3) and (A4), we have

$$Y_t - mY_{t-1} = A \qquad \text{(A5)}$$

The next step is to find that level of income $\bar{Y}$ which, *if* it obtained in period 0, would obtain for ever after: this is called *equilibrium income*. $\bar{Y}$ will clearly be obtained by putting $Y_t = Y_{t-1} = \bar{Y}$ in (A5). We get

$$\bar{Y} - m\bar{Y} = A \quad \text{or} \quad \bar{Y} = \frac{A}{1-m} \qquad \text{(A6)}$$

the familiar Keynesian multiplier expression.

Now let us consider the general case where Y_0 is not necessarily equal to $\bar{Y}$. We want to find out what happens to income as time goes on.

Define $y_t = Y_t - \bar{Y}$. Then y_t is the deviation of period t income from equilibrium income. If we now subtract (A6) from (A5) we get

26

$$y_t - m y_{t-1} = 0 \qquad \text{(A7)}$$

Thus
$$y_1 = m y_0$$
$$y_2 = m y_1 = m^2 y_0$$
$$y_3 = m y_2 = m^3 y_0$$

and so on. Thus for each t, $y_t = m^t y_0$. Now recalling the definition of y_t, we get

$$Y_t = \bar{Y} + m^t (Y_0 - \bar{Y})$$

Since $0 < m < 1$, m^t will become very small as t becomes large. So as time goes on, Y_t approaches $\bar{Y}$.

The above merely formalises what every good elementary textbook says about the multiplier. However, the reader is invited to study the 'formalities' carefully before progressing further.

MODEL B. AN INVENTORY-CYCLE MODEL

Our assumptions are as follows:

Consumption function
$$C_t = a + m Y_{t-1} \quad (0 < m < 1) \qquad \text{(B1)}$$

Investment function
$$I_t = \bar{I} \quad \text{(a positive constant)} \qquad \text{(B2)}$$

Output determination
$$Y_t = Y_{t-1} + r(\bar{S} - S_t) \quad (r, \bar{S} \text{ positive constants}) \qquad \text{(B3)}$$

Stock accumulation
$$S_t - S_{t-1} = Y_{t-1} - Z_{t-1} \qquad \text{(B4)}$$

Note that (B1) and (B2) are identical to (A1) and (A2) respectively. Setting $Z_t = C_t + I_t$ and $A = a + \bar{I}$ as before, we have

$$Z_t = A + m Y_{t-1} \qquad \text{(B5)}$$

The main difference between Models A and B lies in the output-determination equation. We assume for the purposes

27

of Model B that producers do not respond instantaneously to demand but rather desire in the long run to carry over a constant quantity $\bar{S}$ of stocks (or 'inventories') from period to period. They attempt to adjust towards this as follows. Let S_t be the *actual* quantity of stocks at the *beginning* of period t. Then if S_t happens to be equal to the desired quantity $\bar{S}$, firms simply continue production at the level of the previous period; if, on the other hand, S_t falls short of (exceeds) $\bar{S}$ then, we assume, production is increased (diminished) from period $(t-1)$ to period t, by an amount proportional to the size of the stock-discrepancy, $\bar{S} - S_t$. This assumption is written down as equation (B3) with r measuring the speed of stock-adjustment.

Equation (B4) expresses the assumption that all demands are met *either* out of current production *or* out of stocks (in particular, stocks do not run out); the net excess $(Y_{t-1} - Z_{t-1})$ of production over demand during period $t-1$ will then be equal to net stock accumulation during that period, which is identically equal to $S_t - S_{t-1}$.

Having set up and explained the assumptions of the model, let us investigate their implications for the behaviour of Y_t. Let us first 'lag' (B3) by one period (i.e. replace t by $t-1$ throughout) and subtract the resulting equation from (B3) itself: We obtain

$$Y_t - Y_{t-1} = Y_{t-1} - Y_{t-2} - r(S_t - S_{t-1}) \qquad \text{(B6)}$$

Eliminating $(S_t - S_{t-1})$ between (B4) and (B6), we obtain

$$Y_t - (2-r)Y_{t-1} + Y_{t-2} = rZ_{t-1} \qquad \text{(B7)}$$

If we now lag (B5) by one period and eliminate Z_{t-1} between the resulting equation and (B7) we obtain

$$Y_t - (2-r)Y_{t-1} + (1-rm)Y_{t-2} = rA \qquad \text{(B8)}$$

Note now an important difference between (B8) and (A5): in Model B, unlike Model A, income is determined by its values in the preceding *two* periods. Equation (B8) is therefore known as a *second-order difference equation*.

Because of the second-order nature of Model B, we must, in this model, define equilibrium income to be that income level

28

$\bar{Y}$ which, if it obtained in the first *two* periods, would be maintained thereafter. By (B8) $\bar{Y}$ is given by

$$\bar{Y} - (2-r)\bar{Y} + (1-rm)\bar{Y} = rA \qquad \text{(B9)}$$

Since $1 - 2 + r + 1 - rm = r(1-m)$, we have

$$\bar{Y} = \frac{A}{1-m}$$

as before.

Again as before we set $y_t = Y_t - \bar{Y}$ and subtract (B9) from (B8) to obtain

$$y_t - (2-r)y_{t-1} + (1-rm)y_{t-2} = 0 \qquad \text{(B10)}$$

We cannot solve this 'by eye' as we could (A7). A mathematical digression is therefore necessary: the relevant formulae, which will be stated without proof, are important and quite easy to remember.

DIGRESSION ON SECOND-ORDER DIFFERENCE EQUATIONS

Consider the equation

$$y_t + by_{t-1} + cy_{t-2} = 0$$

where b, c are constants and the values of y_t at $t = 0$ and at $t = 1$ are given 'initial conditions'. In the economic examples, y_t is interpreted as the *deviation of income from equilibrium income*; the truth of the mathematical results does not, of course, depend on this interpretation.

The results shortly to be given are concerned with what happens to y_t as t becomes large. This may strike the careful reader as being illicit; having stressed the fact that we are dealing only with short-run models, we are now suddenly talking about the behaviour of y_t as t approaches infinity. Unfortunately this is inevitable. The behaviour of y_t in the first few periods will be heavily dependent upon the initial conditions; the only general results we can hope for concern what happens after

29

sufficient time has elapsed for the 'dominant' tendencies to make themselves felt.

We now classify the eventual behaviour of y_t, according to the various values of b and c. Throughout the following discussion, since y is the deviation from equilibrium income, *'stability' will mean that y_t approaches zero as t becomes large, 'instability' that it does not.* Other terminology will be explained as we go along.

(1) If

$$b^2 > 4c \quad \text{and} \quad b < 0 \quad \text{and} \quad -b + \sqrt{(b^2 - 4c)} < 2$$

we have *monotonic stability;* as t becomes larger, y_t steadily approaches 0 either from above (as i

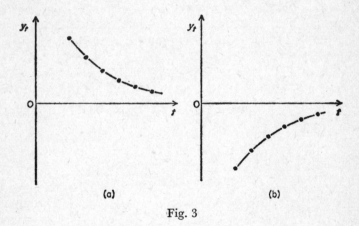

(a)   (b)

Fig. 3

(as in Fig. 3(b)); which situation occurs depends on initial conditions.

(2) If

$$b^2 > 4c \quad \text{and} \quad b < 0 \quad \text{and} \quad -b + \sqrt{(b^2 - 4c)} > 2$$

we have *monotonic instability:* y_t moves cumulatively away from 0 either upward (Fig. 4(a)) or downward (Fig. 4(b)) depending on initial conditions.

(3) If

$$b^2 > 4c \quad \text{and} \quad b > 0 \quad \text{and} \quad +b + \sqrt{(b^2 - 4c)} < 2$$

30

we have *stability with alternations* (Fig. 5); y_t approaches 0, switching each period from positive to negative or vice versa.

(4) If

$$b^2 > 4c \quad \text{and} \quad b > 0 \quad \text{and} \quad +b + \sqrt{(b^2 - 4c)} > 2$$

we have *instability with alternations* (Fig. 6): as in Case (3), y_t switches sign each period, but for any large positive number

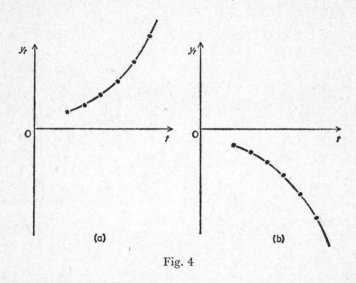

(a)   (b)

Fig. 4

M (say, 1000) there will exist an *infinite* sequence of values of t (say 71, 73, 75....) for which $y_t > M$ (and another infinite sequence for which $y_t < -M$).

(5) If

$$b^2 < 4c \quad \text{and} \quad c < 1$$

we have *stability with oscillations* (Fig. 7). This is just like Case (3) except that y_t takes more than one period to change sign: therein lies the difference between oscillations and alternations. The oscillations are here said to be *damped*.

(6) If

$$b^2 < 4c \quad \text{and} \quad c > 1$$

31

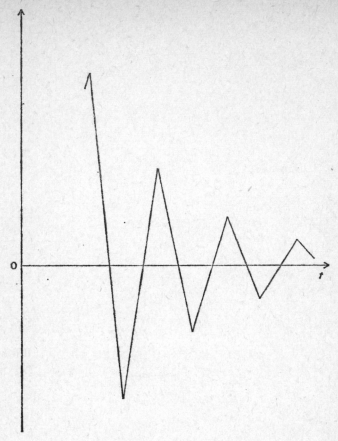

Fig. 5

we have *instability with oscillations* (Fig. 8). This bears the same relation to Case (4) as (5) does to (3). The oscillations here are said to be *explosive*.

Note that we have *stability* in Cases (1), (3) and (5); *instability* in Cases (2), (4) and (6).

The results just stated can be summarised in the 'Baumol diagram', Fig. 9. This illustrates which values of b and c correspond to each of the Cases (1) through (6). The diagram is constructed as follows: Measure c along the horizontal axis, b along the vertical. Draw the curve $b^2 = 4c$. This runs through

32

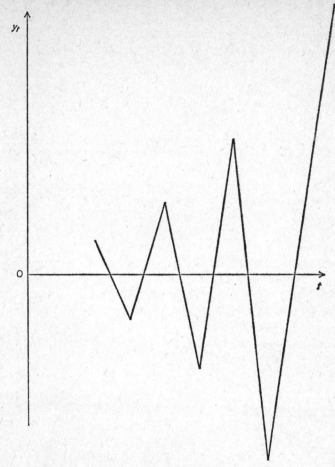

Fig. 6

the points $c = 1$, $b = 2$ and $c = 1$, $b = -2$. Join these points with a straight line and draw lines from each to the point $c = -1$, b = 0. The regions corresponding to the Cases (1) through (6) can then be marked off as shown.

The attentive reader will have noticed that we have not dealt with 'boundary cases' like $b^2 = 4c$ or $b = 0$. These cases can be investigated by using intuition or any book on difference equations, preferably in that order.

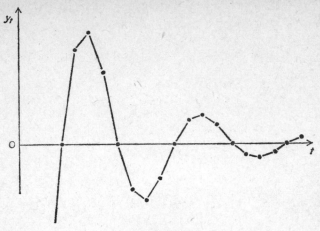

Fig. 7

Before moving on, we should introduce a small *caveat* about initial conditions. Obviously if y_0 and y_1 both happen to be exactly zero, then y_t will also be zero for all t, regardless of which of the cases (1) through (6) holds true. Also, and this is more subtle, it *may* happen in case (2) or (4) that if the ratio of y_1 to y_0 is 'exactly right' (i.e. takes *one* particular value), then

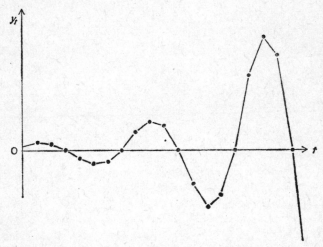

Fig. 8

there will be stability rather than instability. Apart from these odd cases (and notice that the oddity here pertains to initial conditions, not to the values of b and c), the results given above are quite general.

We now derive a simple theorem which is extremely useful for economic applications.

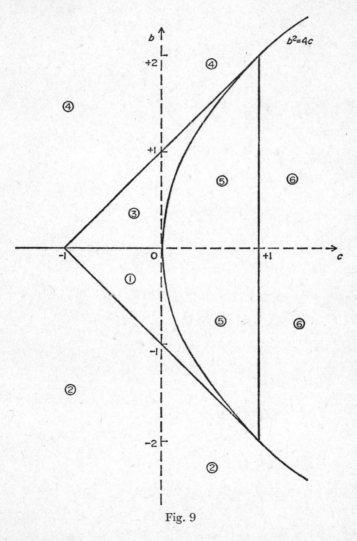

Fig. 9

THEOREM. Suppose that $b < 0$ and $1+b+c > 0$. Then we have stability (either monotonic or with oscillations) if $c < 1$, and instability (either monotonic or with oscillations) if $c > 1$.

Proof. Consider Fig. 9. The condition $b < 0$ rules out cases (3) and (4). The condition $1+b+c > 0$ implies that we cannot be in that part of region (2) to the left of the line $c = 1$. Hence if $c < 1$ we must be in region (1) or (5), while if $c > 1$ we must be in region (2) or (6). This is the required result.

We are now equipped to return to economics.

CONTINUATION OF MODEL B

From (B10) $(y_t + b y_{t-1} + c y_{t-2} = 0)$

where $b = r-2$, $c = 1-rm$.

Since r and m are both positive, $c < 1$. Also $1+b+c = r(1-m) > 0$, since $r > 0$ and $m < 1$. Further, b will be negative provided that $r < 2$ (i.e. provided firms do not 'violently overshoot' when adjusting for stock-discrepancies). Under these conditions, it follows from the Theorem that the time path of y_t displays either monotonic stability or damped oscillations, so that income will approach $\hat{Y}$ in either a steady or an oscillatory manner.

The necessary and sufficient condition for oscillations may here be written $(r-2)^2 < 4(1-rm)$. Since $r > 0$, this is equivalent to $r < 4(1-m)$. For example, if $r = 0.6$ and $m = 0.8$ the path to equilibrium displays damped oscillations.

MODEL C. THE MULTIPLIER–ACCELERATOR MODEL

There are several variants of this famous model: the one given here is perhaps the most familiar version:

Consumption function

$$C_t = a + m Y_{t-1} \quad (0 < m < 1) \tag{C1}$$

Investment function

$$I_t = \bar{I} + v(\Upsilon_{t-1} - \Upsilon_{t-2}) \quad (v > 0) \tag{C2}$$

Output determination

$$\Upsilon_t = Z_t \tag{C3}$$

This is exactly like Model A except for the acceleration term in the investment equation (C2). This is not the place to discuss whether the accelerator gives a 'good' theory of investment; the issue is briefly mentioned in Chapter 4 (for further discussion see Junankar [29]).

Simple manipulations show that

$$\Upsilon_t - (m+v)\Upsilon_{t-1} + v\Upsilon_{t-2} = A \tag{C4}$$

where $A = a + I$ as usual. Again as usual, equilibrium income $\bar{\Upsilon}$ is given by

$$\bar{\Upsilon} = A/(1-m)$$

and the deviation $y_t = \Upsilon_t - \bar{\Upsilon}$ of income from equilibrium satisfies the second-order difference equation

$$\Upsilon_t + by_{t-1} + cy_{t-2} = 0$$

where, here,

$$b = -(m+v) \quad \text{and} \quad c = v.$$

Since m and v are positive, $b < 0$, while $1 + b + c = 1 - m > 0$. Applying the Theorem we see that y_t approaches zero if and only if $v < 1$.

The condition for oscillations reduces here to the inequality $(m+v)^2 < 4v$, which may be shown to be equivalent to $\{1 - \sqrt{(1-m)}\}^2 < v < \{1 + \sqrt{(1-m)}\}^2$.

Our results may be summarised as follows:

(i) If v is small [to be precise, if $v < \{1 - \sqrt{(1-m)}\}^2$], y_t approaches $\bar{\Upsilon}$ steadily.

(ii) If v is slightly less than 1 [to be precise, if $\{1 - \sqrt{(1-m)}\}^2 < v < 1$] then Υ_t approaches $\bar{\Upsilon}$ in an oscillatory fashion, the deviation y_t experiencing damped oscillations.

(iii) If v is slightly greater than 1 [to be precise, if $1 < v < \{1 + \sqrt{(1-m)}\}^2$], then Υ_t oscillates explosively about $\bar{\Upsilon}$.

(iv) If v is large [to be precise, if $v > \{1+\sqrt{(1-m)}\}^2$], then Υ_t moves cumulatively away from $\bar{\Upsilon}$.

A numerical example: suppose that $m = 0\cdot84$ so that $\sqrt{(1-m)} = \sqrt{(0\cdot16)} = 0\cdot4$, $\{1+\sqrt{(1-m)}\}^2 = 1\cdot4^2 = 1\cdot96$, $\{1-\sqrt{(1-m)}\}^2 = 0\cdot36$. Then if $0 < v < 0\cdot36$, we have monotonic stability; if $0\cdot36 < v < 1$, we have damped oscillations; if $1 < v < 1\cdot96$ we have explosive oscillations and if $v > 1\cdot96$ we have monotonic instability.

What happens (for general m) when $v = 1$? This is the dividing line between damped and explosive oscillations. As one might expect, one gets the situation depicted in Fig. 10, where

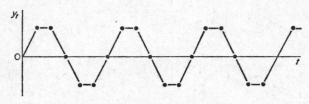

Fig. 10

the oscillations neither explode nor decay: the excess of peak income over equilibrium income remains constant, peak after peak. But this very special case with v exactly equal to one, is the *only* case of Model C which exhibits such regular cyclical behaviour; if v were to fall ever so slightly below 1, the oscillations would die away, albeit slowly. There is clearly something unsatisfactory about this for the trade-cycle theorist, and we shall attempt to come to grips with this problem in the next chapter.

We conclude this chapter with two variants of Model C. If we postulate that consumption depends on *current* income, that the accelerator relationship is *unlagged*, but that output adjusts to demand with a one-period lag, we obtain the model

$$C_t = a + m\Upsilon_t,$$
$$I_t = \bar{I} + v(\Upsilon_t - \Upsilon_{t-1}),$$
$$\Upsilon_t = \mathcal{Z}_{t-1}$$

This yields a difference equation in income identical to (C4).

38

If on the other hand we postulate the unlagged consumption and investment functions of this amended model, while postulating the instantaneous-adjustment output-determination equation $Y_t = Z_t$, we obtain a model which is 'bogus', and for this reason can yield absurd results. The reader is invited to verify this by considering the case where $m = v$ and Y_0 is not equal to A/v.

Guide to further reading
The most famous account of multiplier–accelerator interaction is Samuelson [44]; for the theory of inventory cycles see Metzler [37].

If the reader finds the mathematics of the last chapter difficult, this is probably not because of unfamiliarity with the difference equation concept, but because of lack of facility with basic algebraic manipulations, particularly those involving inequalities; in that case he will find chapter 1 of Ferrar [14] helpful. An extensive discussion of difference equations in economics is given in Part I of Gandolfo [18].

3 Ceilings, Floors and Contra-cyclical Policies

This chapter discusses some more variants of the 'multiplier–accelerator interaction model' introduced as Model C in Chapter 2. We first describe a cycle theory, due essentially to Hicks, which has the theoretically attractive property of implying regular cycles in income, which neither explode nor die away. We then return to the original model and discuss what would be the effect on income, in an economy obeying the 'laws' of the model, of various government policies.

A 'CEILING-AND-FLOOR' THEORY OF THE CYCLE

In Model C, the difference equation telling the story of how income changed from period to period was of the form

$$y_t + b y_{t-1} + c y_{t-2} = 0$$

where y_t was the *deviation* of income from equilibrium income

$$\bar{Y} = A/(1-m)$$

It turned out that only in the special case where c ($=$ acceleration coefficient v) was exactly 1, would one get oscillations which were neither damped nor explosive. This is a special case of the following result: given any difference equation of the form

$$y_t + b_1 y_{t-1} + b_2 y_{t-2} + \ldots + b_k y_{t-k} = 0$$

the only values of the coefficients which lead to non-explosive, non-damped oscillations in y_t will be such that a small change, be it ever so slight, in the coefficients will lead y_t either to approach zero or to behave explosively as time goes on.

The source, then, of the awkward finding at the end of the last chapter lies not in the fact that only three periods ($t, t-1$ and $t-2$) were relevant for the equations, still less in some mysterious intrinsic property of the accelerator. The reason why cycles, if any, were either explosive or damped except in a very special case was that the model was *linear* and *deterministic*: all functions of Y_{t-1} and Y_{t-2} which appeared were of the simple form

$$b_0 + b_1 Y_{t-1} + b_2 Y_{t-2}$$

and no probabilities or random variations were involved. Recent work, discussed later in this book, brings in random variations explicitly; the Hicksian approach introduced here keeps things deterministic, but is essentially non-linear.

The model to be discussed modifies Model C of the last chapter as follows: the system 'normally' behaves like Model C, with coefficients which would, in the absence of the modifications, make the behaviour of income *unstable;* the acceleration coefficient v is assumed to be considerably greater than 1. However, we postulate an upper limit (or *ceiling*) to *income* and a lower limit (or *floor*) to *investment*. We shall assume that both these values are constant over time. (Hicks's original formulation and most subsequent work assumes a positive trend rate of growth. However, the main analytical points can be made without this complication).

Before setting up the model, we introduce a little mathematical notation. Given two numbers x and y we define

$$\max(x,y) = \begin{cases} x \text{ if } x > y \\ y \text{ if } x \leq y \end{cases}$$

and

$$\min(x,y) = \begin{cases} y \text{ if } x > y \\ x \text{ if } x \leq y \end{cases}$$

Thus, for example, $\max(3,4) = 4$, $\min(3,4) = 3$, $\max(-2,-4) = -2$, $\min(5,-1) = -1$, $\max(8,8) = 8$.

The model now runs as follows:

44

Consumption function
$$C_t = a + mY_{t-1} \quad (0 < m < 1) \tag{1}$$

Investment function
$$I_t = \max(\bar{I} + v(Y_{t-1} - Y_{t-2}), I^f) \quad (v > 1, 0 < I^f < \bar{I}) \tag{2}$$

Output determination
$$Y_t = \min(C_t + I_t, Y^p) \tag{3}$$

The consumption function is therefore as in Model C.

The investment function works as follows: I_t is determined by the same relation as in Model C, *provided* the resulting quantity of investment does not fall below some minimal quantity I^f, determined by long-term commitments (and replacement, if we interpret Y as *gross* income). The statement that $I^f < \bar{I}$ implies that the accelerator relation will determine I_t for some negative values of $Y_{t-1} - Y_{t-2}$, *provided* that Y_{t-2} did not exceed Y_{t-1} by more than the quantity.

$$B = \frac{\bar{I} - I^f}{v}$$

I_t is plotted against $(Y_{t-1} - Y_{t-2})$ in Fig. 11. The resulting function is clearly *non-linear*, with a kink at the point $(-B, I^f)$.

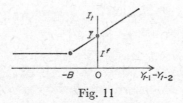

Fig. 11

Consider the output-determination equation (3). Suppose there exists some maximal level of output Y^p determined by labour supply, limitational quantities of capital goods, and possibly by external factors. As long as aggregate demand $Z_t = C_t + I_t$ does not exceed Y^p, output is assumed to respond instantaneously to demand. If, on the other hand, Z_t exceeds Y^p then current output is Y^p and demands in excess of that are satisfied out of stocks, or not at all.

45

Now let us see what happens to income over time.

Let $\bar{Y} = \dfrac{A}{1-m}$ where $A = a + \bar{I}$.

We assume that $Y^p < \bar{Y}$; $\bar{Y}$ will then be equilibrium income. (Why is this so? Why does it depend on Y^p exceeding $\bar{Y}$? And a question to bear in mind in reading the next few paragraphs: what would happen if $\bar{Y}$ were greater than Y^p?)

Now suppose $Y_1 > Y_0 > \bar{Y}$ and consider the economy as from period 2. Given the fundamental instability (v much greater than 1) we see that at time S, say, income hits its ceiling value Y^p. We now show that the economy can remain on the ceiling for *at most* two periods.

If $Y_{s+1} < Y^p$ then the economy remains on the ceiling for but one period (namely, s) and the result is trivial. So it remains to show that if $Y_s = Y_{s+1} = Y^p$ then $Y_{s+2} < Y^p$.

In this case we have

$$C_{s+2} = a + m Y_{s+1} = a + m Y^p$$

and $I_{s+2} = \bar{I} + v(Y_{s+1} - Y_s) = \bar{I} + v(Y^p - Y^p) = \bar{I}$

Adding

$$Z_{s+2} = C_{s+2} + I_{s+2} = a + m Y^p + \bar{I}$$

By the definition of $\bar{Y}$ we have $a + \bar{I} = (1-m)\bar{Y}$,

so $Z_{s+2} = m Y^p + (1-m)\bar{Y}$,

or $Y^p - Z_{s+2} = (1-m)(Y^p - \bar{Y})$ (4)

Now m, the marginal propensity to consume, is assumed to be less than 1, while $\bar{Y} < Y^p$ by assumption. The right-hand side of (4) is thus the product of two positive terms and is therefore positive. Thus $Z_{s+2} < Y^p$. But then by (3), $Y_{s+2} = Z_{s+2}$ and $Y_{s+2} < Y^p$ as required.

We now see that income can remain at its ceiling Y^p for at most two periods. Having come off the ceiling, income falls at an increasing rate; this follows from the 'basic instability' assumption. There therefore comes a time, say u, such that $Y_{u-1} - Y_{u-2}$ is less than the negative number $-B$.

Thus at the time u, investment is stripped to its bare essentials, the 'basic commitment' quantity I^f. By (2), therefore, the

46

accelerator switches off and the equations describing the economy are now

$$C_t = a + m\varUpsilon_{t-1}, \qquad I_t = I^f, \qquad \varUpsilon_t = C_t + I_t$$

This is, of course, identical with Model A of the last chapter, save that I has been replaced by the smaller quantity I^f. Income will therefore tend steadily towards $\varUpsilon^f = (a + I^f)/(1 - m)$.

But income never actually reaches $\varUpsilon^f$. For while income falls after time u, and may at first do so rapidly, *the rate of decrease* of income declines as time goes on. For as $\varUpsilon_t$ approaches $\varUpsilon^f$, so (one period behind) does $\varUpsilon_{t-1}$ and similarly so does $\varUpsilon_{t-2}$. Thus $\varUpsilon_{t-1} - \varUpsilon_{t-2}$ approaches $\varUpsilon^f - \varUpsilon^f = 0$. Explicitly, the analysis of Model A shows that in this case

$$\varUpsilon_{t-1} - \varUpsilon_{t-2} = (1 - m)m^{t-u-2}(\varUpsilon^f - \varUpsilon_u)$$

which, while negative, climbs steadily towards zero as t increases.

There therefore must come a time $w(\, > u)$ such that

$$\varUpsilon_{w-1} - \varUpsilon_{w-2} > -B$$

This, of course, is the signal for the accelerator to take over again: income rises, consumption follows, income increases yet again, investment increases and the whole process starts over again.

Two cycles are illustrated in Fig. 12.

The above argument is of some intricacy. In particular, the reader may find the explanation of the lower turning point somewhat difficult; it is an example of what is known in mathematics as a limit argument, and these are always tricky. What is vitally important to appreciate is the asymmetry between the

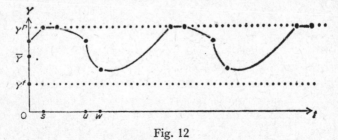

Fig. 12

two turning points. Income bounces off the ceiling; it does *not* bounce off the floor Y^f, indeed it never gets there. *Investment* does reach *its* floor and indeed may stay there for a considerable part of the contraction phase of the cycle. *Income*, on the other hand, rolls gently down towards Y^f but is pulled up by the accelerator before getting there.

While a considerable theoretical advance, this model does not appear to be a particularly good explanation of the trade cycle in western economies, at any rate during this century. Victor Zarnowitz of the N.B.E.R., in a summary of the work of Wesley Mitchell and his associates and successors at that institution over a period of forty years, writes ([52] p.18):

> ... the expansionary and contractionary processes, while 'cumulative', are usually self-limiting due to the stresses and imbalances that they themselves create; they are rarely terminated by any identifiable barriers. Thus, the economy is definitely not viewed as fundamentally unstable in the sense of generating potentially 'explosive' fluctuations which are constrained by some limiting factors.

The key phrase here is 'potentially explosive'; the evidence both from National Bureau research and from econometric models (of which more in the next chapter) simply does not bear out the fundamental instability postulated in the model. One quite fallacious argument to the effect that it does, goes as follows. Consider a 'typical' advanced economy where the capital–output ratio is three years (that capital–output ratios are measured in years surprises some students; it should not. Capital is measured in constant-price pounds, output in constant-price pounds *per year*; the result follows immediately). Suppose we maintain that the acceleration coefficient v is identical to the capital–output ratio. Then if the unit period is one year, v will be 3; if it is a quarter, $v = 12$; if it is a month we have $v = 36$. In each case v is considerably in excess of 1, so we have the instability postulated.

The fallacy here lies in equating the parameter 'v' in the model with the capital–output ratio. To do this, we must first assume that *all* investment is accelerator-induced. Second, we must assume that the model 'represents reality' in the

48

sense that we can really believe that all relevant behaviour lags are of one or two periods. Neither of these is reasonable. Why then operate with these simple models? Simply because they give a useful idea of the sort of things that can and cannot happen, and because they are useful for pouring cold water on naive ideas (as will become abundantly clear in the second half of this chapter). If we want a model which can really tell us something about a particular country's economic experiences, there is no alternative to econometric estimation of more complex systems, using real data.

None of this denies, of course, that economic expansion can be blocked by some kind of 'ceiling' (think of the repeated British balance-of-payments crises in the 1950s and early 1960s), still less the historical platitude that contractions have in fact ended in finite time. What is being maintained is that the mathematically neat model just described is not a very helpful way of explaining such phenomena.

GOVERNMENT POLICY IN THE MULTIPLIER–ACCELERATOR MODEL

Consider an 'economy' where the behaviour of national income Y_t over time is described by an equation of the form

$$Y_t + bY_{t-1} + cY_{t-2} = Q \tag{5}$$

where b, c and Q are constants with $1 + b + c > 0$ and $Q > 0$. Two examples of such an equation are (B10) and (C4) of Chapter 2, referring respectively to Models B and C. In such an economy equilibrium income $\bar{Y}$ is given by

$$\bar{Y} = Q/(1 + b + c)$$

and the behaviour over time of $y_t = Y_t - \bar{Y}$ is given by

$$y_t + by_{t-1} + cy_{t-2} = 0 \tag{6}$$

Now consider the effects of a change in the value of one or more of the 'parameters', b, c and Q. Such a change may be brought about by spontaneous once-and-for-all shifts in the

49

conduct of households or firms or, as we shall see, by government policy.

The effects of the change will, in general, be of two kinds. First, the *equilibrium* level of income may be affected. In the context of government policy there is an extensive body of literature on this type of effect, involving such concepts as the balanced-budget multiplier. This is *not* our concern here: indeed we shall consider only parameter changes which are 'neutral' in the sense that they leave equilibrium income unaltered. For example, suppose that b is *raised* to b^*, with c unchanged; then we shall assume that this is offset with respect to equilibrium income by an increase of Q to Q^*, where

$$\frac{Q^*}{1+b^*+c} = \frac{Q}{1+b+c}$$

Second, changes in the parameters will affect the *time-path of actual income*, even in the absence of any change in equilibrium income. It is this effect which we shall study in detail.

Suppose that income is approaching its equilibrium value, via damped oscillations. Suppose there occurs a change in the parameters which, while leaving equilibrium income at its original value, changes the path along which income approaches equilibrium. We wish to find out precisely how such changes in b and c affect the behaviour of Y_t in equation (6).

To do this, we reconsider the 'Baumol diagram' of Fig. 9, which is reproduced as Fig. 13. Suppose that the original situation gives values of b and c represented by point P_0 in the diagram, giving damped oscillations. What happens if we increase b, i.e. move northward in the diagram to the point P_1? The answer is, oscillations will be damped as before, and the damping will be at the same rate as before (i.e. it will take just as long as in the old situation for y to get into a position where it *stays* within a given distance from 0); however, the oscillations will be *more frequent* than before. The easiest way to see this is to consider what happens if we move b all the way up to $2\sqrt{c_0}$; at that point we are on the boundary between oscillations and alternations, in other words oscillations are as frequent as they could possibly be. Similarly a southward move from P_0 to P_2

50

will keep the rate of damping unchanged but will make oscillations *less* frequent (indeed, if we reduce b all the way to $-2\sqrt{c_0}$ we reach the boundary between damped oscillations and monotonic stability; in other words we encounter damped cycles whose peak-to-peak length approaches infinity).

An eastward shift from P_0 to P_3 will, on the other hand, keep

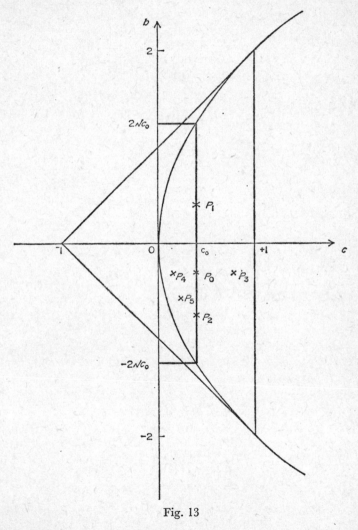

Fig. 13

the frequency of oscillations unchanged, but will *reduce* the rate of damping; fluctuations will therefore occur as frequently as in the *status quo*, but will be larger in size ('of greater amplitude' is the technical term); in other words, the peak value of y in each cycle will be greater under the new regime than under the old, and the trough value correspondingly less – this of course assumes that we start from identical initial y_0 and y_1, under the two regimes compared. To see this, again consider the extreme case where c is increased to 1. There, damping is abolished altogether, and y_t ceases to approach 0 over time; this of course means that if c is only slightly below 1, damping will be very slow. Similarly, a westward move from P_0 to P_4 implies cycles more heavily damped than at P_0.

A shift from P_0 which is neither horizontal nor vertical can be regarded as a combination of a horizontal shift and a vertical one. For example, the southwest shift from P_0 to P_5 implies milder, less frequent cycles at P_5 than at P_0.

Now let us return to our multiplier–accelerator model. We may write down the equation for income for Model C in the form

$$Y_t + bY_{t-1} + cY_{t-2} = A_t$$

where
$$b = -(m+v)$$
$$c = v$$

and
$$A_t = A \quad \text{(constant for all } t\text{)}$$

Call this the *status quo*, and suppose that it leads to damped oscillations. We now consider various government policies which make government expenditure react to previous income (previous, since any policy takes time to put into effect, and there is, of course, an information lag between economic events and the government's appraisal thereof). Such policies may be represented by letting A_t (which may be taken to include government expenditure) be not constant over time, but depend on Y_{t-1}, Y_{t-2}, etc.

> *Policy (i)* The government, in an attempt to counteract the cycle, makes government expenditure depend *negatively* on last period's income.

Hence we have

52

$$A_t = E_1 - q\Upsilon_{t-1} \quad (E_1 > 0, q > 0)$$

In order for this to be a 'neutral shift' relative to the *status quo*, E_1 has to have a specific value relative to the other parameters. It is easy to see that this requires

$$E_1 = A + q\bar{\Upsilon}$$

The equation determining income is now

$$\Upsilon_t + b\Upsilon_{t-1} + c\Upsilon_{t-2} = E_1 - q\Upsilon_{t-1}$$

or
$$\Upsilon_t + (b+q)\Upsilon_{t-1} + c\Upsilon_{t-2} = E_1$$

Letting
$$y_t = \Upsilon_t - \bar{\Upsilon}$$

we have
$$y_t + b_1 y_{t-1} + c_1 y_{t-2} = 0$$

where
$$b_1 = b + q$$
$$c_1 = c$$

Thus, relative to the *status quo* represented by equation (C4) in the last chapter, we have a northward shift in the Baumol diagram. Thus cycles are neither more nor less damped than before, and oscillations are more frequent. This is not a particularly desirable outcome from such a seemingly helpful 'counter-cyclical' policy. However, there is worse to come.

Policy (ii) As (i) but with a two-period lag.

Here
$$A_t = E_2 - q\Upsilon_{t-2} \quad (E_2 > 0, q > 0)$$

For neutrality
$$E_2 = A + q\bar{\Upsilon}$$

Letting
$$y_t = \Upsilon_t - \bar{\Upsilon}$$

and operating as above,

$$y_t + b_2 y_{t-1} + c_2 y_{t-2} = 0$$

where
$$b_2 = b$$
$$c_2 = c + q$$

This is an 'eastward' shift on the Baumol diagram. The cycles are of the same length as in the *status quo* but less damped – oscillations are of greater amplitude, and income approaches equilibrium less rapidly. For anyone who values macro-economic stability, the results of this policy are unambiguously bad.

It is worthwhile to stress that this is by no means an obvious result. If the normal length of the trade cycle is $2n$ periods from peak to peak, and if the government deflates the economy n

periods after each peak and reflates it n periods after each trough, it will, of course, aggravate the existing cycle. But the result just derived is much more sophisticated than this. The lag of policy (ii) is two periods, while the peak-to-peak length of the cycle both before and after the imposition of the policy is *greater* than four periods, perhaps considerably so; for the length of the cycle would be four periods only if b were zero; since a southward shift in the Baumol diagram implies a reduction in the frequency of cycles, the fact that b is negative (being equal to $-m-v$) implies a cycle *more* than four periods in length.

Policy (iii) The government attempts to stabilise the economy by setting government expenditure *high* if income has recently been *rising, low* if it has been *falling*.

Here we have $A_t = E_3 - q(Y_{t-1} - Y_{t-2})$ $(q > 0)$

Neutrality here requires $E_3 = A$. Obviously the effects of the policy are identical to those of a *reduction* of the accelerator from v to $v-q$, so that b rises from $(-m-v)$ to $(q-m-v)$ and c falls from v to $v-q$.

Thus the effects of this policy are mixed. By reducing c, the policy makes the oscillations in income more heavily damped; cycles become smaller more quickly. Because of the increase in b, however, fluctuations are more frequent with the policy than without it.

Taxation can be introduced into Model C as follows:
Suppose tax payments T (*net* of transfers) are related to income Y by:

$$T = T_0 + xY$$

where T_0 and x are constants: x is the *marginal* rate of income taxation. Then making other assumptions as before we can write down Model C with m and a interpreted respectively as

$$m = (1-x)m_0 \quad \text{and} \quad a = a_0 - mT_0$$

where a_0 and m_0 are constants: m_0 is here the marginal propensity to consume out of *disposable* income.

Now consider the effect of a once-and-for-all increase in the progressiveness of income taxation. Let the marginal tax rate

54

x be raised, and let this be accompanied by a *reduction* in T_0 sufficient to keep the equilibrium level of income unchanged. How will this affect the dynamics of the system?

Clearly, the effect is that of a *decrease* in the marginal propensity to consume out of total income. Thus m declines, and b increases, leaving c unchanged. This is identical to the effect of Policy (i); fluctuations are made more frequent by the imposition of the policy; the speed with which income, once disturbed from equilibrium, will return thereto, is unchanged.

What would be an unambiguously good policy *in this model?* By 'good' we mean one which increases damping and makes fluctuations less frequent: that is, a policy which reduces both b and c. Comparing Policy (iii) with the *negative* of the effect of a high marginal rate of tax, we see that one 'good' policy would be one in which government expenditure at time t was negatively related to $(Y_{t-1} - Y_{t-2})$ and in which the marginal rate of tax was kept *low* (!)

All this, of course, refers to one very stylised theoretical model. It is certainly not the author's intention to advocate regressive income taxation for contra-cyclical or any other reason. The purpose is purely negative; the above examples are surely more than enough to show that 'common-sense' or 'intuitive' statements about the efficacy of 'automatic stabilisers' simply will not stand up to rigorous analysis. The effects of a particular type of 'stabilisation' policy depend crucially on the time-lags involved both in the implementation of the policy itself, and in the private-sector decisions which the policy is intended to influence. To investigate these in a real economy, we have to bring theory and fact together, via econometric models; these will be discussed in the next chapter.

Guide to further reading

Hicks's trade-cycle model is explained in [26] and developed further in [25]. A variant of the ceiling–floor model in which the economy may, in certain circumstances, stay on the ceiling with persistent excess demand is discussed by Matthews [34].

For a detailed account of the implications of multiplier–accelerator interaction for stabilisation policy, see Baumol [7].

Note that the tools used above for analysing the dynamics of fiscal policy can also be used to discuss monetary policy – by, for example, generalising Model C to the case where investment depends on (lagged) interest rates as well as acceleration effects. One such analysis is presented in Lovell and Prescott [33].

4 The Econometric Approach

The previous two chapters should not be regarded as a summary of a 'theory' of the cycle; a more apt description would be 'an analysis of some logical constructions which at one time or another have been believed to provide an explanation of the trade cycle, but which on closer inspection probably do not'. Thus some writers still refer to 'the multiplier–accelerator theory of the cycle', but as a matter of simple mathematics, multiplier–accelerator interaction is neither necessary nor sufficient to give rise to oscillations and will *not* give rise to self-generating oscillations, without damping or explosion, except in a very particular case.

Similarly the second part of Chapter 3 can hardly be regarded as 'the theory of stabilisation policy'. Indeed, it points out, in the context of a very simple model, how very little we can say about policies of a given qualitative character without detailed knowledge of the time lags involved in their operation.

What all this adds up to is that a faith in some simple causal mechanism which, when revealed, will enable us to understand all, is probably a chimera as far as cycles (and many other economic phenomena) are concerned. Probably more can be gained by detailed study of particular economies, and for this we need an interaction of fact and theory. Such an interaction is provided by econometric models.

An econometric model is a set of equations describing the behaviour over time of an economy (or of a sector or market therein). These equations are of two types: accounting identities, and so-called 'structural equations'. The structural equations may be classified as 'behavioural' (for example, consumption functions), 'technical' (production functions), or 'institutional' (tax revenue equations).

The equations involve two sorts of quantity: 'variables' such as national income, consumption or population which are the data of the model, are measured by consulting national accounts or other official statistics, and naturally vary over time; and 'parameters' which are assumed for the purposes of the model to remain constant over time, which cannot be observed directly, but can be *estimated* by the model builder once he has collected his data and set up his model. More will be said shortly on the role of parameters; for the present they may be regarded as the empirical man's counterpart to the elasticities, marginal propensities, et cetera of economic theory.

Let us now consider further the 'variables' of an econometric model. There are two kinds of variable: 'endogenous' variables which are explained by the model, and 'exogenous' ones which are not. The model tells the story of what determines the values of the endogenous variables; part of this story concerns the impact on the endogenous variables of the exogenous ones, but there is no explanation *in the model* of why the exogenous variables took the values they did. Consider as an illustration an econometric model of a single market, say for potatoes: price, and quantity sold, of potatoes will be endogenous variables; consumers' income, price of certain other commodities and climatic conditions will be typical exogenous variables, affecting but not affected by the endogenous ones.

It should, however, be emphasised that the econometrician's choice of the variables to appear in the model, and of the form of the relationships between them are, in the last analysis, a matter of *opinion*; this is an inevitable consequence of the fact that the economist's data are not generated by a controlled experiment! In particular, a model-builder's choice of which variables to treat as exogenous and which as endogenous will be influenced by his theoretical perspective, as well as by the purposes for which his model is to be used. For example, the money supply is treated as an exogenous variable in some models of entire economies and as an endogenous one in others.

A typical structural equation in an econometric model is the following consumption function:

$$C_t = a_0 + a_1 Y_t + a_2 Y_{t-1} + a_3 C_{t-1} + a_4 N_t + u_t$$

Here C_t is consumption in period t, Y_t income, N_t population. Thus we see that the model 'specifies' that the value at time t of the endogenous variable consumption depends on the (presumably endogenous) variable T_t on the *lagged-endogenous* variables Y_{t-1} and C_{t-1} and on the (presumably exogenous) variable population. The numbers a_0, a_1, ... a_4 are the parameters of the consumption function in this model and can be estimated by any of a number of statistical techniques.

The term u_t at the end of the consumption equation above is called the 'error' or 'disturbance' term. This expresses the fact that we cannot expect any set of equations to describe *exactly* the dynamic path of an economy; rather, each structural equation of an econometric model expresses a relation which is in part deterministic, but also disturbed by other factors which are collectively thought to be subject to a law of chance. The term u_t is the random part of consumption; just how important this is (in other words, how wide is the band in which consumption in period t could quite plausibly lie, *given* values of the *variables* on the right-hand side of the equation) may be measured by estimating statistically the standard deviation of the probability distribution of u_t.

Econometric models have been built and estimated for most western countries; indeed there are numerous competing ones for the United States and for some other countries. The length of the unit period in these models is generally either one year or one quarter, though Professor Ta-Chung Liu of Cornell University has constructed a monthly model of the United States economy [32].

The time-span of observations for most national annual econometric models starts in the late 1940s, though some U.S. models are based on data beginning in the late 1920s. Quarterly models generally start later; the period of observations for the F.M.P. model of the United States, with emphasis on the effects of the monetary mechanism on the 'real' economy, starts in 1956. ('F' stands for Federal Reserve Board, 'M' for Massachusetts Institute of Technology, 'P' for the University of Pennsylvania; see the paper by Ando and Modigliani [6] for an excellent account of the model and its uses.)

The size of the models varies greatly, from four equations to over four hundred. Little can be said at a very general level about whether large models are 'better' than small ones; it depends what one wants to use the model for. As we shall see, some small models give quite good summary descriptions of how major aggregates behaved during their period of observation. On the other hand, there are some purposes for which more complicated structures are essential: if one wants to predict how the additional spending generated by a given cut in the personal income tax would be split into expenditure on food, non-food non-durable consumption, motor cars, other durables, housing, et cetera, one has no choice but to work with a large model (but notice that there is always a danger that very large models will be too unwieldy to do this sort of job effectively; see R. J. Gordon [20]). Also, the institutional and indeed geographical characteristics of a particular national economy will influence the number of equations necessary to model it; for example, a national econometric model which ignores foreign trade is obviously a more sensible proposition for the United States than for the Netherlands.

Before we leave generalities and discuss the uses of econometric models, two points of a more sophisticated nature should be made. The first concerns the nature of 'variables'. It is probably fair to say that most of the relationships postulated by economic theory, whether macro or micro, axiomatic or informal, are phrased in terms of quantities which are not directly observable, *even in principle*, in any economy we know. Examples of such quantities are 'labour input', 'the' interest rate, and 'net non-human wealth'; notice that only in the first of these is the measurement problem an index-number problem in the usual sense. On the other hand, the economic statistics used to define variables in econometric models are collected for a variety of reasons, mostly quite unconnected with economic analysis. It should therefore be emphasised that the structural equations of an econometric model are relationships between observable quantities suggested by economic theory, rather than direct expressions of theoretical propositions. This distinction raises serious methodological problems, whenever econometric models are used to test theories; more generally, it serves as a reminder that model-building is an activity requiring the exercise of judgement, not just of deriving the correct conclusions from accepted 'laws' of economic theory and mathematical statistics.

As a final general point, note that most econometric models have a dynamic structure that is 'bogus' rather than truly dynamic in the sense of Chapter 2; endogenous variables at a given time are jointly dependent. This is inevitable in annual models and may make sense in quarterly models, the idea being to capture the effect of lags in behaviour shorter than the unit period of the model. It is also germane to mention that even if the unit period is short, so that *some* kind of truly-dynamic model is feasible, *two or more* alternative causal structures may suggest themselves, and the model-builder may have no way of discriminating between them (compare Model C of Chapter 2 with the *first* variant thereof described on p. 38). The statistical problems raised by the approximation of truly-dynamic models by 'bogus' ones are difficult and have not, to this author's knowledge, been completely resolved. (These issues are discussed, at a very advanced level, in [47].)

Econometric models have many uses; among these are the quantitative appraisal of economic policies, the analysis of trade cycles and, of course, forecasting. This is not the place to discuss the alternative forms of forecast which may be made with the help of an econometric model, save to point out that the ability of a model to predict reliably is widely regarded as the most appropriate test of its worth as a description of an economy, and that in recent years econometric forecasts, while inevitably imperfect, have performed respectably in comparison with predictions generated by other systematic methods.

The remainder of this chapter is devoted to the use of econometric models in investigating cyclical fluctuations. Suppose we have an econometric model of an economy; suppose we make 'plausible' assumptions about the behaviour over time of the exogenous variables; our problem is, does this stylised picture of the economy indicate a natural tendency for endogenous variables, income in particular, to move in cycles?

Three ways of approaching this problem will be described, and some results of their application discussed. The first two of these methods, which will be labelled 'the analytical method'

63

and 'non-stochastic simulation', consider what would happen if the economy behaved in the manner depicted by the model, with parameter values as estimated, *but with all disturbance terms set equal to zero:* the third method, 'stochastic simulation', explicitly introduces the random disturbances (the adjective 'stochastic' is a synonym for 'random').

The 'analytical' method is based on a generalisation of the mathematical results stated without proof in Chapter 2, whereby the evaluation of certain functions of the coefficients of a second-order difference equation enable one to classify the eventual behaviour of the system as monotonic stability, explosive oscillations, or whatever. Now even comparatively small econometric models will of course lead to difference equations in income of order higher than two: Y_t will depend not only on Y_{t-1} and Y_{t-2} but also on Y_{t-3}, Y_{t-4} and so on. It is nevertheless the case that if the model is relatively simple (linear or approximately so) then evaluation of appropriate functions of the parameters (these being set at their estimated values) will yield all relevant information about the eventual behaviour of the endogenous variables, given suitably simple assumptions about the behaviour of the exogenous ones. Two features of this method should be stressed: first, its validity depends crucially on the assumption that disturbance terms may be set equal to zero; second, while the calculations it requires present no difficulties of mathematical principle, the computational difficulties may be severe.

Bert Hickman [23] applied this analytical method to a large selection of econometric models for ten different countries. For all but two models, one for Australia and one for Italy, he found monotonic stability, corresponding to Region (1) of Fig. 9 (p. 30). In the Australian and Italian cases, the analytical method implied damped oscillations.

Gregory Chow has developed in three papers ([12], [11], [13]; in order of publication) a very elementary and yet powerful model for the United States. This model only uses four endogenous variables: consumption (generated by a lagged consumption function), investment (determined by a version of the acceleration principle incorporating interest-rate effects), income (identically equal to the sum of the first two plus exogenous expenditure), and the interest rate (determined by what is essentially the *LM* curve of the macro-economics textbooks, with the money supply treated as an exogenous variable). Some complications were, of course, necessary to make the model operational; an (exogenous) price index was used to convert purported relationships between 'real' magnitudes into estimable equations in terms of 'nominal' (current-price) variables; also the lags in Chow's consumption and investment equations are a little more complicated than those discussed earlier in this book. None the less Chow's four-equation model has very much the spirit of the models discussed in Chapters 2 and 3 of this book, in its simplicity and in its total neglect of the 'supply side'; there are *no* labour supply functions and *no* production functions, and there is no use of input–output information. Perhaps surprisingly, in view of these remarks, the estimated model fitted United States annual data remarkably well for the period 1929–63, particularly with respect to the acceleration equation for investment. Applying the 'analytical' method, Chow discovered that his model predicted monotonic stability in $Y_t - Y_{t-1}$, in other words, a *stable linear trend* in annual income.

Simulation methods, which may be used for forecasting and policy evaluation as well as for the analysis of cycles, work as follows. One feeds into a computer suitable *initial* values of the endogenous variables and, for the entire economic epoch to be simulated, values of the exogenous variables. If the epoch is located in the past the values of the exogenous variables may either be invented (if, for example, one wants to find out what would have happened had government policies been different) *or* those which actually occurred (this is useful for evaluating forecasts); if one is interested in the future, one has no choice but to invent values. Disturbance terms are either set equal to zero (this is *non-stochastic* simulation) or (in *stochastic* simulation) generated via a normal random number programme according to the probability laws assumed in the specification of the model, with standard deviations as estimated in the process of estimating the parameters. With this information, the computer generates hypothetical 'histories' of the endogenous variables.

There are two reasons for using non-stochastic simulation

rather than the 'analytical' method of Hickman and Chow in cases where the disturbance terms are set equal to zero. First, models with elaborate production and investment functions do not possess a simple enough mathematical structure for the analytical method to be feasible. Second, the analytical method, like the results of Chapter 2 which it generalises, can only predict the eventual behaviour of a system, and that only under very simple assumptions about the exogenous variables; if we are more interested in short-run behaviour, simulation becomes necessary.

Zarnowitz and associates ([53], [54]) applied non-stochastic simulation to four large models of the United States economy. Simulations were made both of the 'past', to try to find out what *would* have happened if the economy had behaved like the model in question, with exogenous variables taking the values they in fact took, *but with disturbance terms equal to zero*, and of the future, using plausible guesses at the values of the exogenous variables. For both types of simulation they found strong indications of stability. With respect to the former: 'common to both short and long non-stochastic simulations is a strong tendency to underestimate the amplitudes of the observed cyclical movements' ([54] p. 527). For the latter: 'the non-stochastic simulations for future periods...produce smooth trend-dominated series with recurrent, if damped, fluctuations. Thus these models do not generate cyclical movement endogenously' ([54] p. 528).

This impression of stability seems to be a common result of non-stochastic work with econometric models. But when we turn to *stochastic* simulation, which allows specifically for the random disturbance terms, a different picture emerges.

The classical study of cycles along these lines is the article by Irma and Frank Adelman [5] on the dynamic properties of the 25-equation model of the United States economy constructed by L. R. Klein and A. S. Goldberger. The Adelmans first applied non-stochastic simulation, assuming steady linear trends for the exogenous variables: the result was monotonic stability. This was confirmed by an investigation of the results (according to the model without disturbance terms) of a large cut in federal government expenditure. The next step was to apply simulation with 'Type I random shocks': that is, the simulation was still non-stochastic in the sense that the random disturbance terms *in the equations* were ignored, but the *exogenous variables* were assumed to be in part generated by a random process. The result of this was to produce three-to-four-year cycles, but of an amplitude too small to be a plausible picture of the National Bureau cycle. Finally the Adelmans introduced 'Type II shocks', in other words stochastic simulation proper. The effect of allowing the disturbances in the equations to play a role was a sequence of fluctuations showing 'startling agreement with the National Bureau cycle'.

More recent applications of stochastic simulation have also shown a tendency for models which display little or no oscillation when the disturbances are left out to display cycles when the disturbances are put in. It should, however, be pointed out that recent simulations on large models of the United States (see, for example, [53]) give more realistic-looking pictures of cyclical behaviour when the disturbances for successive time periods are correlated with each other.

These results are not totally surprising. The fact that a basically stable linear system can generate regular cycles when perturbed by random shocks has been known by statisticians for a long time; indeed, a famous article by Ragnar Frisch [17] applied this result to trade-cycle analysis as long ago as 1933. The important point to notice is that the cycles emerge from the *interaction* of the model with the random disturbances; it is the *relationships of the model* which 'process' the shocks in such a way as to make income move in cycles. The action of random shocks alone would not produce anything like the pattern observed (there is plenty of evidence for this: see as a recent example Howrey's tests in [27] p. 622).

What are we to conclude from this survey of models? At first it does seem that deterministic income–expenditure models which generate oscillations that are unstable, only slightly damped, or constrained as in the ceiling–floor model, do *not* give a plausible explanation of the quantitative feature of cyclical behaviour in advanced economies. This does not, of course, rule out the possibility that theoretical models, involving no shocks, may give a plausible explanation of long swings; similarly it may be true that radically new insights may give a better explanation of the short cycle than anything discussed in this book. What does seem to be correct is that, given our present knowledge and the existing corpus of macro-economics, the picture of a fundamentally stable system subject to random shocks is more accurate than that of a highly unstable system with or without them.

But where do the shocks come from? Clearly shocks directly affecting the size of exogenous variables (for example sudden increases in exports, or changes in government policy) play some part in this, but equally clearly *this is not the whole story*; for recall Zarnowitz's results that non-stochastic simulation, given exogenous variables as they actually occurred, under-estimated the extent of actual fluctuation, and that the Adelmans were unable to produce National Bureau type cycles using Type I shocks alone. Rather, the shocks which appear to be crucial are the disturbance terms in the structural equations of the models: in other words, the random components in the relations determining the endogenous variables; in the model used by the Adelmans, these random components were most important in the equations determining fixed investment and business saving. These shocks may be interpreted as evidence of the importance of unpredictable and unsustained changes in mood or taste within the private sector, or as an indication that the model itself has failed to take into account some important feature of the economy.

But whether the source of 'shocks' is the volatility of government policy, the state of confidence or economists' ignorance, it appears that at the present state of knowledge such random disturbances have to be taken into account in investigations of economic fluctuations. This has implications for the analysis of economic policy: some research on these lines is discussed in the last chapter of this book.

Guide to further reading
Probably the most important of the econometric articles referred to in the text is I. and F. Adelman [5]; it is not excessively technical and the reader is urged to consult it.

For an elementary introduction to econometric models with particular reference to forecasting, see Suits [48]. A very clear and thorough comparison of the forecasting performance of a sophisticated econometric model with that of a method making no use of economic theory has recently been given by Nelson [39].

One aspect of the econometric approach to trade cycles which has not been treated here is the application of *spectral analysis*. This statistical technique (a simple account of which is given in Wonnacott and Wonnacott [50] pp. 477–92) searches for the inherent cyclical properties either of a series of observations or of a hypothetical random process. It may be used to analyse both observed economic time series and the probabilistic nature of the behaviour of endogenous variables of a model, as implied by given estimates of parameters and assumptions about the disturbances. See Howrey [28] for examples of the first type of research and Chow [11], Chow and Levitan [13] and Howrey [27] for examples of the second.

5 Monetary Aspects

In this chapter we consider the cyclical behaviour of the money supply. Throughout the chapter, M denotes the money stock, and Y national income at *current prices* ('money income' or 'nominal income' for short). 'Velocity' V, or more correctly the income velocity of money, is simply *defined* to be the ratio of Y to M; it is not a concept implying a particular view of the world.

Why should we be interested in *nominal* income? Is not trade-cycle analysis primarily concerned with 'real' quantities like industrial production and *constant-price* G.N.P.? Yes, indeed, and if the price level moved over time in a large-amplitude cycle unrelated to the trade cycle, then statements about peaks and troughs in money income would have no implication for those in real income. But in fact, the general experience in industrial countries has been for price levels to move cyclically, so that money income has in fact moved with the cycle, displaying larger amplitude than real income.

We start with some facts. These are entirely concerned with the United States, for it is in that country, thanks largely to the heroic labours of Professor Milton Friedman and his colleagues at the University of Chicago and the National Bureau of Economic Research, that most systematic empirical work on money and cycles has been done.

Over the seventy years from 1870 to 1940, the *average* rate of increase of the money stock was considerably higher than that of money income; indeed, V fell from 4·5 in 1870 to below 2 in 1940. V declined sharply during the Second World War, but has steadily increased since then.

This process has not been smooth, for both M and Y have undergone cyclical fluctuations. Indeed Y, V and (with some qualification) M have tended to move *with* the cycle.

During those cycles in which the contraction in real and money income was not severe, there was no *absolute* decline in the money stock during the contraction, and indeed, little cyclical change in the rate of growth of the money stock. In 'deep depression' cycles (for example those leading to the severe contractions of 1892–4 and 1929–33) the money stock moved cyclically, with very approximate coincidence of cycle peaks with peaks in the stock of money; however money stock, *adjusted for time trend*, leads money and real income by about five months, and the rate of growth of M leads the level of Y by as much as 16 months and the rate of growth of Y by a shorter interval. 'A leads B' means here, as usual, that cyclical peaks in A precede those in B, and similarly for troughs.

On the other hand, during all these cycles, the amplitude of the movements in money income exceeds those in money. Indeed, together with movements of M, there occurred cyclical movements in V – these accounting for approximately equal proportions of the movement in Y (note that this is a statement of fact, not a hypothesis about causality). The evidence on velocity may thus be summarised as follows: over the entire period, Y increased, and M increased proportionately *more*; but during cyclical expansions of Y, M increased at a slower rate than Y; the direction of difference between the long-run growth rates is largely due to the fact that M was declining slowly in those periods when Y was declining rapidly, and increasing when Y was stagnating.

The size of a nation's money stock depends in the first instance on one stock and two ratios: the total quantity of currency and bank reserves, the *actual* (not legal–maximum) ratio of deposits to reserves held by banks, and the deposit–currency ratio of the non-bank public (see Rowan [43] chapter 15). It appears that changes in the deposit–currency ratio have been the most important source of changes in the money stock. Nevertheless policy changes initiated by the authorities have on numerous occasions had a marked effect on the money stock; and such spontaneous changes, when they have taken the form of a contraction in the money stock, have often foreshadowed a contraction in money income: examples are the contractions of 1920–1 and 1937–8.

74

What can be inferred from these facts, and from a more detailed study of monetary behaviour in particular cycles? A first point is that the 'old-quantity-theory' proposition that V can be treated as a constant for the purpose of short-run analysis is decisively refuted. Second, it seems clear from analysis of particular episodes that money does have a strong independent influence on income: for example, a more sensible policy by the Federal Reserve, especially after Britain left the gold standard, could have done much to mitigate the horrors of the Great Depression. A third point is the strong reverse influence of changes in income (or more generally, business conditions in the private sector) on the money stock, via changes in the deposit–currency ratio.

Note, incidentally, that the 'lead' of trend-adjusted M over Y, and of the rate of change in M over the rate of change of Y is not in itself an indication of a causal influence of money on income. First, the fact that the rate of change of M has a long lead over the level of Y is of no great interest: it is a mathematical fact that, given any time series A which oscillates in a regular ('sinusoidal' to be precise) fashion, the rate of change of A will lead A itself by a quarter of a cycle. So, given cycles in Y, the long lead of the rate of change of M over the *level* of Y is largely an arithmetical consequence of the short lead of the rate of change of M over the rate of change of Y. Note that there is no theoretical reason for a direct relationship between Y and the rate of change of M; the fact that they are of the same dimension (both measured in dollars per year) is quite irrelevant, since all monetary theory deals with the interaction of flows (such as Y), with stocks (such as the level of M). As Friedman and Schwartz put it ([16] p. 163; page references are to the Penguin reprint):

The central element in the transmission mechanism...is the concept of cyclical fluctuations as the outcome of balance sheet adjustments, as the effects on flows of adjustments, between actual and desired stocks. It is this interconnection of stocks and flows that stretches the effect of shocks out in time, produces a diffusion over different economic categories, and gives rise to cyclical fluctuations.

75

Further, it is not even true that the slight lead of the *level* of trend-adjusted M over the *level* of Y, and of the rate of change of M over the rate of change of Y, is necessarily evidence of a causal link *from* money *to* income. Indeed, Tobin [49] has shown that such leads may occur in a simple theoretical model in which such a causal link is ruled out by hypothesis, the authorities being assumed to expand and contract the money supply so as to 'meet the needs of trade' at an imposed interest rate. In Tobin's model the factor crucial in producing the lead effect is the pro-cyclical movement in the government's budget surplus.

This counter-example is important, not because the model is a plausible picture of the world (it is not, and Tobin stresses this point), but because it shows that facts about timing are unlikely to be very good evidence *for* a particular causal hypothesis, simply because a given timing sequence may be logically consistent with so many widely different explanations that it fails to support any of them. Evidence about leads and lags *can*, however, provide reasons for *rejecting* theories, as we shall see shortly.

But now let us accept that money has a strong independent influence on money income. Can we go from this proposition to a *theory* of fluctuations, at any rate in nominal income, in which money stock is the prime mover and taxes and government expenditure (and *a fortiori* any expenditure aggregate, such as consumption and investment, affected thereby) are *in themselves* irrelevant? Such a theory of fluctuations would have to do two things. First, it would have to work out the effects of changes in the money stock on changes in money income; second, it would have to give some indication of what sort of behaviour of the monetary authorities (possibly subject to random disturbances) would, together with the effects just mentioned, be sufficient to generate cycles.

Now no monetarist has (to this writer's knowledge) attempted the second part of this programme; the above quotation from Friedman and Schwartz can perhaps be taken as a statement of faith that this can be done. Indeed only tentative steps have been taken with respect to the first part. But let us see what issues are involved. Consider the *ISLM* analysis of the macro-economics textbooks (Rowan [43] chapter 12): assume that the *IS* curve is downward-sloping rather than vertical (expenditure is interest-elastic) and that the *LM* curve is upward-sloping rather than horizontal (neither the demand for nor the supply of money is *infinitely* interest-elastic). Then certainly increases in the money stock will increase income, while lowering interest rates.

But there is nothing specifically 'monetarist' about this; indeed, most econometric models allow for this effect. The question at issue is whether we can *concentrate* on the monetary sources of fluctuations in income, to the virtual exclusion of the effects of autonomous changes in expenditure flows.

Two justifications could be offered for such a simplification: we may call them the 'weak' and the 'strong' hypotheses. The weak hypothesis maintains that, while alternative histories of private investment or government fiscal policy *could* have led to sizeable cyclical fluctuations in the American economy, the fluctuations in income that *in fact* took place may be ascribed to changes in the money stock; proponents of the weak hypothesis would therefore represent the nature of changes in United States income on the *ISLM* diagram by allowing the *LM* curve to shift while keeping the *IS* curve stationary. The trouble with this is that it implies *counter-cyclical* movement of interest rates and of velocity, and such movements did not happen; we shall return to the velocity evidence later.

The strong hypothesis justifies a concentration on monetary influences by postulating that autonomous changes in expenditure (in particular, private investment) not only have not had, but could not have had, significant effects on money income. Let us consider the theoretical basis for this view.

The usual post-Keynesian account of the effects of an autonomous but sustained increase in investment runs as follows. Income increases via the multiplier, and this causes the transactions demand for money to increase. With excess demand in the money market, interest rates will rise. This will exert downward pressure on investment (and possibly consumption) expenditure and hence on income. But the very fact that interest rates have risen implies that there is lower excess demand for money at any given level of income; this can come about *either* via a non-zero interest-elasticity of demand for money, *or* via a non-zero interest-elasticity of supply of money, or, of course, via both. Thus, in order to choke off the excess demand for money, the rate of interest does not have to increase by an amount sufficient to reduce income to its old value. Instead, the shift in the investment schedule enables the economy to sustain a higher level of income (and of interest rates) than before.

There are two cases where the conclusion 'more income' will fail to follow from the postulate increase in investment. They may be labelled 'vertical *LM*' and 'horizontal *IS*'. The first case is usually associated with 'quantity theory' or 'monetarists', but some of Friedman's recent writings suggest the second. In the 'vertical LM' case, the demand for and supply of money are interest-inelastic, so that the rise in interest rates required to choke off the excess demand for money in the above example is indeed sufficient to drive income down to its old level; or, more generally, the desire to hold more money occasioned by the rise in expenditure and income causes people to try to sell assets, and the resulting decline in the prices of these assets causes in turn a reversion of income to its old level. In the 'horizontal *IS*' case, on the other hand, the demand for money *does* depend on interest rates, but the interest rate itself is essentially unaffected by fiscal policy or autonomous expenditure, presumably because of an extremely *high* interest-elasticity of investment demand. In this case, the story told in the last paragraph comes to an abrupt halt at an early stage: the tiny rise in interest rates caused by the sale (or attempted sale) of the first hundred consols brings about a decline in investment so massive as to annihilate the initial stimulus.

Econometric evidence on expenditure and money-market functions does not lend support to either special case; indeed, much of the controversy about the interest-elasticity of the demand for investment has been about whether this elasticity is *zero*, not infinity! But let us waive these objections and consider whether either of these special cases is compatible with the evidence on cycles presented at the beginning of this chapter.

Consider the contrast between long-run and short-run

movements in velocity. This is of course quite incompatible with 'vertical *LM*' *in its crude form*. But Friedman has a way round this [15]. Suppose that the supply of money is exogenously determined, and that the demand for money depends on 'permanent income', this being a weighted average of past incomes (say, the average of this year's income, last year's and that of the year before). Then the cyclical time-path of permanent income will be smoother than that of Y, so that the amplitude of cycles in Y, say A, will be greater than the amplitude of cycles in permanent income, which amplitude we call B.

Now suppose that the elasticity of demand money with respect to permanent income is greater than one. This is, of course, consistent with the long-run decline in velocity as M and Y both rose. It also means that cyclical changes in M will be accompanied by cyclical changes in permanent income of smaller amplitude; letting C be the amplitude of cyclical fluctuations in M, we have C greater than B. But if A is three times as great as B, while C is only 1·5 times as great as B, then A will be twice as great as C; and *this* is consistent with the short-run pro-cyclical movements in velocity!

But as Tobin [49] has pointed out, this account is quite inconsistent with the evidence of *timing* of money and income in the cycle. For if we are to assume that money supply is exogenous, and money demand depends on permanent income alone, then in order to provide a sufficient increase in *permanent* income to 'accommodate' a large injection of M, current income Y would have to undergo a sudden and large increase; and this initial overreaction would induce in subsequent periods an overestimate of permanent income, an excessive demand for money, and thus downward pressure on income, *even while M was still rising*. Thus Y would already be falling by the time M reached its peak; M lags behind Y in other words. More precise analysis of this model (see [49]) leads to the result that the rate of change of M would lag considerably behind the rate of change of Y, and have only a short lead over the level of Y. This is clearly contrary to the facts.

So much for 'vertical *LM*'. What about 'horizontal *IS*'? Here, the supply of and demand for money can be assumed to be interest-elastic, so the *proximate* explanation of the cyclical movement in velocity is the usual Keynesian one: interest rates move cyclically, and velocity depends positively on interest rates. But *why*, given horizontal *IS* curves, do interest rates move cyclically? Why do *horizontal IS* curves shift up and down over the cycle? Not, by hypothesis, because of random-shock or accelerator-induced changes in investment or fiscal stimuli or drags: all of these would be represented by horizontal displacements in the *IS* curve if that curve were vertical or downward-sloping, but it is not possible to horizontally displace a horizontal (infinite) line. Why then? I do not know.

To sum up: nobody has claimed that 'money is all that matters'. The position of Friedman and the monetarists is, it seems, that the determinants of money income are money, the forces considered in neo-classical micro-economics and growth theory, and institutional and legal factors, but *not* Keynesian effective demand processes and fiscal policies. With regard to cyclical fluctuations, the monetarists do not claim to have a complete theory of the cycle, but have sought elements of an explanation of cycles embodying the proposition that changes in the rate of growth of the money stock are

> a *necessary and sufficient* condition for appreciable changes in the rate of growth of money income ([16] p. 144; my italics).

The present writer confesses that he finds such a search misguided.

Guide to further reading
The articles by Friedman [15], Friedman and Schwartz [16], and Tobin [49], referred to in this chapter are all well worth reading.

For a clear and succinct critique of monetarism see Samuelson [45].

6 No More Trade Cycles?

Since the Second World War, the trade cycle has undergone a profound change of character. In this final chapter, we outline the main features of this change, and discuss whether 'demise' would be a better word. We then consider whether stabilisation policies have helped or hindered this change, and end with a few remarks about the relevance of the econometric approach of Chapter 4 to the formulation of satisfactory stabilisation policies.

If it is asked what the question 'Is the Business Cycle Obsolete?' really means, it can be interpreted roughly as follows: 'Is the British economy ever again going to land in the mess it was in during the early 1930s?' But this is really far too *general* a reply.

Consider in particular the unemployment rate. We all know that governments of civilised countries have for thirty years been committed to the maintenance of full employment, and a good thing too. But this statement about the intentions of governments does beg two rather important questions. First, no government in a mixed economy can keep the unemployment rate at *exactly* zero, or 0·5 per cent, all of the time; there will inevitably be fluctuations in the unemployment rate. This implies that the 'maintenance' of 'full' employment has two aspects: a low *average* rate of unemployment, and little tendency for the rate to deviate much from the average. For example, in the simple models of the second half of Chapter 3, it was assumed that the equilibrium level of output, around which the actual level oscillated, was at a level considered desirable, and the sole function of stabilisation policy was to keep the fluctuations small. We saw that this was not a trivial task.

This distinction between the 'mean' and 'standard deviation' aspects of full employment is not mere logic-chopping; quite apart from the possibility that they involve different trade-offs with other targets of policy, they may also require different policy measurements. This brings us to the second question begged in the above statement about 'governments of civilised countries': what exactly can governments do, as opposed to say, about unemployment? On this very basic question there seems to be massive disagreement among economists.

With respect to the damping of fluctuations in unemployment, most economists would say that enlightened fiscal and monetary policies can be of great help, but would argue about precisely what combinations of policies merit the description 'enlightened'. On the long-run unemployment rate there is an even more tangled dispute. One can make a rough distinction between those economists who believe that the average unemployment rate can be kept at a permanently lower level by expansionary monetary and fiscal policies, and those who do not. But within the first camp there is violent disagreement about whether the lower unemployment forthcoming from demand expansion has to be 'bought' at the cost of a higher inflation rate, and over the role of incomes policy. The other camp consists of economists who regard the long-run average unemployment rate as essentially impervious to *monetary and fiscal policy*, but have no common viewpoint on what determines this rate, and what governments can do to alter it. Some talk darkly of automation; others emphasise regional policies; Friedman maintains that the abolition of minimum wage laws would significantly lower United States unemployment, and so on.

The point here is that the reasons for the extremely low unemployment rate in Britain from the 1940s until the late 1960s and the (by inter-war standards) relatively low rates thereafter are not fully understood. In so far as plausible explanations can be offered, they may come from branches of macro-economics outside the scope of this book, or even from outside economics altogether. And what applies to the story of the British unemployment rate applies with even greater emphasis to the general prosperity in western countries since the war. Indeed, once one considers consumption or the wholesale price index, rather than unemployment, a whole new area of ambiguity comes into view; for it is far harder to give a clear summary of the facts about a quantity with a pronounced time trend than for one that merely fluctuates about a level.

To summarise; the mildness of cyclical fluctuations in western countries since the Second World War is only one aspect of the unprecedented prosperity (albeit accompanied by endemic inflation) which these countries have enjoyed during these years. And it is only with that part of the story that we are concerned here.

In western Europe and Japan, the post-war era has been one of almost uninterrupted growth; absolute declines in output from year to year have been extremely rare. In the United States and Canada, there were four short contractions between 1948 and 1961 and another (relatively mild, by historical standards) contraction from 1969 to 1970. But if we look at output *relative* to the growing trend we see that the old cyclical pattern re-emerges. There is one major exception to this, namely that the length of the new style-growth cycle is shorter in most countries than the old one. It should be explained what adjustment for trend implies here. In a cycle-adjusted-for-trend, or 'growth cycle' an expansion is defined to be a period of fast growth, a contraction one of slow growth. Thus a peak of a growth cycle is not one in which the rate of growth of output passes from positive to negative, as in the old trade-cycle definition, but one in which the rate of growth of output passes from above to below its long-run average level; note that this is *not* the same as defining a peak as a period of maximal growth. (For details see Matthews [35]).

But is this adjustment for trend simply a way in which trade-cycle analysts keep themselves employed, after the original subject of their enquiry has passed into oblivion? It seems unlikely. First, in an economy where people expect growth, a decline of the economic growth rate below its 'normal' value may cause the same sorts of political and social reper- cussion as did absolute declines in the past. Second, given these strong growth expectations, an absolute decline in income will be associated with far greater changes in expendi- ture and production plans than any but the most severe con- tractions in the past; so the contemporary economist interested in such adjustments will want to look beyond absolute expansions and contractions. Third, the growth cycle does display strong family resemblances to the cycles of the past.

To give a British example: when one considers amplitudes of present-day cycles in real income, corrected for trend, with those before 1914 computed on a similar basis, one finds no great difference. Matthews, who performed this experiment, reports ([35] p. 104):

> The difference in amplitude between post-war and pre-1914 years is not very great. The difference between upswing and downswing average annual growth rates is actually larger in 1951–64 than in 1872–1914 but the shorter duration of the 1951–64 cycles makes their overall amplitude somewhat less. Therefore, as far as real G.D.P. is concerned, post-war fluctuations have not been so very small by the standards of the past, but they have been much smaller than they were between the wars.

It should be noted, however, that the amplitude of fluctuations in *employment* has been much smaller than in earlier times. More about cyclical changes in employment will be said shortly. It should, however, be pointed out that, in Britain and elsewhere, the smaller fluctuations have something to do with the shortening of the cycle, and lags in the hiring and firing process.

Further, the sequence of events in the behaviour of particular cyclical indicators within each cycle has changed rather little. A particular phenomenon to have persisted is the tendency of labour's share of income generated in the private sector to move *contra-cyclically*: in other words, the ratio of prices to labour costs per unit of output has moved with the cycle, though with a slight lead.

The proximate reason for this is as follows: let P be an index of prices, W of money wages, X of output per manhour. Then unit labour cost is (W/X) so that the ratio of price to unit labour cost is (PX/W). Now what has happened in western countries, at least since the end of the *First* World War, is that strong pro-cyclical movements in X have dominated any reverse movements in (P/W) and this has continued unchanged in more recent years. Specifically changes in output have been associated with smaller proportional changes in manhours, which in turn have been associated with still smaller proportional changes in employment. This is of course quite at variance with the treatment of the demand for labour (in terms of marginal productivity) given in many books on macro-economics. Two factors would seem to be relevant. The first is the 'overhead' character of much labour, even in manufacturing; the second is the large pro-cyclical swings in capital utilisation. Both of these show up in empirical studies, and labour-economists have found plausible explanations for the first in terms of costs of hiring and firing. But why capital utilisation should be so volatile, and *why the effects on labour productivity should be in the observed direction*, is something which has yet to receive a convincing theoretical justification (in an idealised competitive economy in which 'capital' consists of discrete machines of different specifications, a decline in output would imply a laying-off of machines on which labour was *least* productive).

With respect to prices and wages themselves, the changes have been more marked. It appears that, in the past, money wages *increased fastest* during the latter stages of an expansion, which would help to account for the peak of (PX/W) being reached before that of output. Prices tended to move cyclically. In the inflationary economies of more recent years, things appear to have changed. In the United States it is the *rate of growth* of the price level that has been associated with the *level* of output, though with a slight lead. In the United Kingdom, at least up to the mid-1960s, the price level (*adjusted for trend*) has appeared to move counter-cyclically: one explanation for this lies in the relationship of prices with normal, rather than current, unit labour costs, and the tendency of productivity to move more strongly with the cycle than does money wages.

We now turn to the question of stabilisation policies. It may well be true that the general climate of prosperity, and the contribution of monetary and fiscal policies to expectations that this would continue, have helped in the moderation of the cycle. It is almost certainly true that the growth of the government sector, in and of itself, has helped market economies to react less violently to random shocks than in previous decades (herein lies the strong element of truth in 'arms-economy' theories of the success of the mixed economy). But when we come to more detailed questions, of the form 'have policies specifically designed to be contra-cyclical actually acted against the cycle?' the picture becomes less clear.

As we saw in Chapter 3, such stabilisation policies may have effects very different from those intended. A typical example of our results there was that, in a simple multiplier–accelerator model, seemingly impeccable contra-cyclical policy acting with a one-period lag would serve merely to increase the frequency of fluctuations without affecting their amplitude. Of course it would be absurd to draw from this mathematical exercise the conclusion that post-war 'stabilisation' policies have been responsible for the increased frequency of cycles and had little other effect; but it does mean we need to be cautious in assessing the effects of such policies.

Some economists in western Europe (and particularly in Britain) have maintained that fiscal and monetary policies have actually destabilised the economies concerned. There are two, not wholly compatible, versions of this. One is the idea of a 'policy cycle'. In its extreme form, this thesis pictures a government as oscillating between worry over investment and/or unemployment, and despair over inflation and/or the balance of payments; it reacts to the former with injections of spending and large tax reliefs to consumers and firms, thereby causing an upturn; to the latter, with deflationary policies, thereby starting a contraction. The second proposition blames governments for amplifying cycles which are already there; in the British case, governments are accused of having intensified inflationary pressures in the upswing, by electorally motivated stimulation of consumption, and to have made contractions more severe by restrictive monetary policy, introduced for balance-of-payments reasons.

The trouble with the first of these 'theories' is that it is rather hard to see whether governments are being blamed for something which is really blameworthy. If it is observed that monetary and fiscal policies are primarily responsible for the turning points in numerous cycles (as they have been in many countries) could this perhaps mean that by adopting these policies governments mitigated cycles which would have been of greater amplitude (though perhaps lower frequency)?

As to the second, it is easier to tell revealing anecdotes about particular episodes than to assess different policies systematically. And, as the reader will have guessed from his study of Chapter 4, by 'systematically' is meant 'in the context of an econometric model, taking random shocks into consideration'.

Little work of this nature has yet been undertaken. An article which may point the way ahead is Haitovsky and Wallace [22]. The object of the exercise is to perform simulations with econometric models, as described in Chapter 4 of this book, under alternative specifications of the 'exogenous' variables corresponding to different fiscal and monetary policies. Random shocks are, of course, built in. Indeed, Haitovsky and Wallace do so in a very careful and imaginative manner. The extra twist here is that they allow both for 'discretionary' and 'non-discretionary' policies; the latter consist simply of the government sticking to rules, like Friedman's famous recommendation of a constant rate of growth of the money supply, through good times and bad: discretionary policies, on the other hand, are explicitly counter-cyclical in that they imply a government response (lagged, in general) to observed economic conditions. Haitovsky and Wallace's tentative results for the United States economy were that, within the class of policies considered, discretionary policies appear to be preferable to non-discretionary ones. Their work also produces the result, by now predictable in this kind of work, that taking the random disturbances into account leads to very different policy conclusions from those to be expected from a deterministic model.

This approach is exciting; to evaluate stabilisation policies we must look behind the façade of their immediate effects to the causes of the cycle. If the causes be random shocks acting through a complex mechanism of behaviour relations and technological factors, then we shall have to consider them directly. As yet, the effects of stabilisation policy on these mechanisms is only beginning to be explored. Further exploration may reveal to us whether the trade cycle can indeed be rendered extinct.

Guide to further reading

For excellent discussions of the post-war trade cycle in the United Kingdom and United States see [35] and [51] respectively.

To keep this book within bounds, I have said little about cyclical movements in income distribution, and nothing about the international transmission of trade cycles. A good article on the former topic is Kuh [31]; and on the latter, Rhomberg [41].

Bibliography

The most useful modern book of readings on trade cycles is

[1] R. A. Gordon and L. R. Klein (eds), *Readings in Business Cycles* (George Allen & Unwin, 1966).

The remaining references are listed alphabetically. Some articles have been multiply reprinted; to save space, at most one reprint reference has been given for each item. Also, some articles have been reprinted in collections of essays by their respective authors. These are marked with an asterisk. For example, [15]* means that reference [15] has been reprinted in M. Friedman, *The Optimum Quantity of Money and Other Essays* (Aldine, 1969).

[2] M. Abramovitz, 'The Nature and Significance of Kuznets Cycles', *Economic Development and Cultural Change* (April 1961). Reprinted in [1].

[3] M. Abramovitz, 'The Passing of the Kuznets Cycle', *Economica* (November 1968).

[4] I. Adelman, 'Long Cycles – Fact or Artifact?', *American Economic Review* (June 1965).

[5] I. and F. Adelman, 'The Dynamic Properties of the Klein–Goldberger Model', *Econometrica* (October 1959). Reprinted in [1].

[6] A. Ando and F. Modigliani, 'Econometric Analysis of Stabilization Policies', *American Economic Review* (May 1969).

[7] W. Baumol, 'Pitfalls in Contracyclical Policies: Some Tools and Results', *Review of Economics and Statistics* (February 1961).

[8] M. Bronfenbrenner (ed.), *Is The Business Cycle Obsolete?* (John Wiley, 1969).

[9]* A. F. Burns, 'Business Cycles', *International Encyclopaedia of the Social Sciences*, vol. ii (Collier–Macmillan, 1968).

93

[10] A. F. Burns and W. C. Mitchell, *Measuring Business Cycles* (N.B.E.R., 1946).

[11] G. C. Chow, 'The Acceleration Principle and the Nature of Business Cycles', *Quarterly Journal of Economics* (August 1968).

[12] G. C. Chow, 'Multiplier, Accelerator and Liquidity Preference in the Determination of National Income in the United States', *Review of Economics and Statistics* (February 1967).

[13] G. C. Chow and R. E. Levitan, 'Nature of Business Cycles Implicit in a Linear Economic Model', *Quarterly Journal of Economics* (August 1969).

[14] W. L. Ferrar, *Calculus for Beginners* (Oxford University Press, 1967).

[15]* M. Friedman, 'The Demand for Money: Some Theoretical and Empirical Results', *Journal of Political Economy* (August 1959). Reprinted in [1].

[16]* M. Friedman and A. J. Schwartz, 'Money and Business Cycles', *Review of Economics and Statistics* (February 1963; supplement). Reprinted in *Money and Banking*, A. A. Walters (ed.) (Penguin, 1973).

[17] R. Frisch, 'Propagation Problems and Impulse Problems in Dynamic Economics', in *Essays in Honour of Gustav Cassel* (George Allen & Unwin, 1933). Reprinted in [1].

[18] G. Gandolfo, *Mathematical Methods and Models in Economic Dynamics* (North-Holland, 1971).

[19] R. A. Gordon, *Business Fluctuations*, 2nd edn (Harper & Row, 1961).

[20] R. J. Gordon, 'The Brookings Model in Action: A Review Article', *Journal of Political Economy* (May/June 1970).

[21] M. J. Habakkuk, 'Fluctuations and Growth in the Nineteenth Century', in *Studies in Economics and Economic History: Essays in Honour of Professor H. M. Robertson*, ed. M. Kooy (Macmillan, 1972).

[22] Y. Haitovsky and N. Wallace, 'A Study of Discretionary and Nondiscretionary Monetary and Fiscal Policies in the Context of Stochastic Macroeconometric Models' in [51].

[23] B. G. Hickman, 'Dynamic Properties of Macroeconometric Models: An International Comparison', in [8].

[24] B. G. Hickman (ed.), *Econometric Models of Cyclical Behavior,* Studies in Income and Wealth, vol. 36 (Columbia University Press, 1972; two vols).

[25] J. R. Hicks, *A Contribution to the Theory of the Trade Cycle* (Oxford University Press, 1950).

[26] J. R. Hicks, 'Mr. Harrod's Dynamic Theory', *Economica* (May 1949). Reprinted in [1].

[27] E. P. Howrey, 'Dynamic Properties of a Condensed Version of the Wharton Model', in [24] vol. 2.

[28] E. P. Howrey, 'A Spectrum Analysis of the Long Swing Hypothesis', *International Economic Review* (June 1968).

[29] P. N. Junankar, *Investment: Theories and Evidence* (Macmillan, 1972).

[30]* T. C. Koopmans, 'Measurement without Theory', *Review of Economic Statistics* (August 1947). Reprinted in [1].

[31] E. Kuh, 'Employment and Income Distribution over the Business Cycle', in *The Brookings Quarterly Econometric Model of the United States,* ed. J. S. Duesenbery *et al.* (North Holland, 1966.)

[32] T. C. Liu, 'A Monthly Recursive Econometric Model of the United States: A Test of Feasibility', *Review of Economics and Statistics* (February 1969).

[33] M. C. Lovell and E. Prescott, 'Money, Multiplier–Accelerator Interaction and the Business Cycle', *Southern Economic Journal* (July 1968).

[34] R. C. O. Matthews, 'A Note on Crawling Along the Ceiling', *Review of Economic Studies* (October 1959).

[35] R. C. O. Matthews, 'Postwar Business Cycles in the United Kingdom', in [8].

[36] R. C. O. Matthews, *The Trade Cycle* (Cambridge University Press, 1959).

[37]* L. A. Metzler, 'The Nature and Stability of Inventory Cycles', *Review of Economic Statistics* (August 1941). Reprinted in [1].

[38] W. C. Mitchell, *Business Cycles: The Problem and its Setting* (N.B.E.R., 1927).

[39] C. R. Nelson, 'The Prediction Performance of the

95

FRB–MIT–PENN Model of the US Economy', *American Economic Review* (December 1972).

[40] P. J. O'Leary and W. Arthur Lewis, 'Secular Swings in Production and Trade 1870–1913', *Manchester School* (May 1955). Reprinted in [1].

[41] R. R. Rhomberg, 'Transmission of Business Fluctuations from Developed to Developing Countries', in [8].

[42] W. W. Rostow, *British Economy of the Nineteenth Century* (Clarendon Press, 1948).

[43] D. C. Rowan, *Output, Inflation and Growth* (Macmillan, 1968; 2nd edn 1974).

[44]* P. A. Samuelson, 'Interactions of the Multiplier Analysis and the Principle of Acceleration', *Review of Economic Statistics* (May 1939). Reprinted in *Macroeconomic Readings,* ed. J. Lindauer (Free Press, 1968).

[45] P. A. Samuelson, 'Monetarism Objectively Evaluated' in *Readings in Economics,* 6th edn, ed. P. A. Samuelson (McGraw-Hill, 1970).

[46] J. A. Schumpeter, *Business Cycles* (McGraw-Hill, 1939; two vols).

[47] R. H. Strotz and H. Wold, 'Recursive vs. Nonrecursive Systems: An Attempt at Synthesis', *Econometrica* (April 1960; three papers).

[48] D. B. Suits, 'Forecasting and Analysis with an Econometric Model', *American Economic Review* (March 1962). Reprinted in [1].

[49]* J. Tobin, 'Money and Income: Post Hoc Ergo Propter Hoc?', *Quarterly Journal of Economics* (May 1970).

[50] T. and R. Wonnacott, *Introductory Statistics for Economics and Business* (John Wiley, 1972).

[51] V. Zarnowitz (ed.), *The Business Cycle Today* (Columbia University Press, 1972).

[52] V. Zarnowitz, 'The Business Cycle Today; An Introduction', in [51].

[53] V. Zarnowitz, 'Econometric Model Simulations and the Cyclical Characteristics of the US Economy', in [51].

[54] V. Zarnowitz, C. Boschan and G. H. Moore, 'Business Cycle Analysis and Econometric Model Simulations', in [24], vol. 1.